Truth Be Told

A Teen Breaks Her Silence

Truth Be Told

A Teen Breaks Her Silence

Mya Joyce

Truth Be Told: A Teen Breaks Her Silence

ISBN: 978-1-949513-07-3

Published by The DP Group, LLC.

This book is dedicated to
my grandparents

Acknowledgments

First, I'd like to thank my grandparents. I am who I am because of them and without them I don't know where I'd be. Thank you to my brother, Jerry, for being my first best friend. I'd also like to thank my mama, Mrs. Holmes; she's the reason this book was even possible. She's the person who helped me to truly realize that I can really do or be anything I want.

You know how they say it takes a village to raise a child? I wish I could name everybody who was, and still is, a part of my village, but I can't because I'd literally be naming people all day, but my village is simply amazing. To my former teachers, my family, my church family, my current friends, and everybody else who has helped along the way, thank you.

Contents

Foreword

Our young people have something to say. Even the quietest of our youth have deep, profound angst that needs an outlet. Mya Joyce has found that outlet. Through the sharing of her story she is releasing years of hurt, pain, anger, and frustration. The trauma of her childhood has caused some setbacks in her life, but when I read her story and listen to the anguish in her voice, I hear a young woman that is destined to turn her pain into a platform.

When I first spoke with Mya about publishing her story, I promised to coach her through the process and see it all the way through. I explained that it would be difficult at times, but if she desired to be a sixteen-year-old author she could certainly accomplish that feat — and she did! Words cannot express how proud I am of Mya Joyce. She did what was previously thought to be impossible. It is my prayer that she encourages millions to break the mold, step out of their comfort zones, and unlock the greatness within!

"Truth Be Told" is a story that can resonate with readers both young and old. Young readers will see a reflection of some of their own issues and teen anxiety, while adults will recall how they struggled through adolescence and survived the hellfire of high school. However, this book takes an even deeper dive. Mya writes from her heart about experiences with bullying, suicidal ideations, and even the painful coping mechanism of cutting. She bares her soul when she reveals the grittiness of life in the care of child protective services and the joy of finally going home to live with her grandparents.

Ultimately, this is a story that speaks to the resiliency of our youth — the ability to bounce back from the toughest of circumstances and come back stronger than ever. "Truth Be Told" took great courage. For example, Mya's transparency regarding the deep-seated anger she has toward her mother is heartbreaking to read, but you can't turn away. We can't turn away from stories like hers because too often the voices of our youth go unheard, as Mya so honestly states in her opening chapter. It is time for us to listen to the sound of our youth. It is a sound of healing. It is a sound of hope. It is a sound that will echo for generations to come because what Mya has done will force someone to look and pay attention to those who have previously been silenced and sent subliminal messages that their voices do not matter.

Here, Mya has exposed the most intimate details of her life. As a result, she is literally speaking her healing into existence. I often say, "the road to recovery is paved with purpose!" Mya has blazed a mighty trail. She has found her purpose and I am excited to see where she goes from here.

Sincerely,

Mary Kaye Holmes, #1 International Best-Selling Author of Stripped: A Journey From Rejection to Redemption

Chapter I

Not Your Average Sixteen-Year-Old

Often, the feelings of teenagers are ignored or viewed as invalid. Our voices often go unheard because adults believe that we're too immature to have real issues and feelings. Unfortunately, what most adults don't think about is how harboring these emotions, and not having any type of way to express them, can negatively impact us. Instead of letting these emotions turn me into an angry, mentally unstable individual, I've decided to write this book and use it as an outlet to come to terms with and live in my truth. This book is my way of facing my trauma head on and becoming free of the negative control my experiences have had over my life.

This book is not only for me but for other teenagers who feel like their voice isn't being heard or that have to keep everything to themselves. Also, I'm writing this for those who have experienced things similar to me and to let them know that it does get better. I want this book to serve as a reminder that any and everything is possible no matter what you've experienced or where you come from — and that it is absolutely okay to be different!

I am not your average sixteen-year-old. When most people look at me today, they see a happy, content, and grateful girl, but I wasn't always like this. In fact, it took several years for me to come out of my shell and gain the little confidence that I have at this moment. You're probably wondering: "What could a girl have possibly been through in sixteen short years of life?" Well, like I said, I'm not your average sixteen-year-old.

Although I haven't been living for a very long time, my life has been riddled with rejection, depression, and one disappointment after another. Although sixteen years may not seem like a long time to some, I have suffered in silence for far too long. It is time for my voice to be heard. It is time for me to be free.

Sadly, the main cause of all these negative emotions was my very own mother. Your mother is supposed to be the one who encourages you the most, right? But what if I told you mine did the exact opposite? Over the years, I've had several encounters with my mother and the majority of them were negative. During almost every conversation we had, my mother was verbally abusive. There were multiple times when my mother called me stupid, ugly, and even fat, which caused me to develop low self-esteem.

In fact, I became accustomed to the constant disrespect, the put-downs, the let-downs, and the disappointment. Sadly, I began to believe all the negative things she said to me. In fact, it would surprise me when she held a normal conversation with me. From the moment I was born she despised me and did very little to hide the fact that she did not want me.

My mother was a drug addict.

There is a certain level of freedom that rushes through me when I say that because most people don't know my story as well as they might think. I've always believed that this was partially my fault because I feel like I'm living a lie by letting people have this false perception of me. For example, my friends at school think I live with my mother and father and that my parents are married. They believe I come from a perfect, God-fearing family. Well, the God-fearing part is true, but we are far from perfect. Whenever I'm around others I'm always happy and they assume I have no problems at all.

For a while I was fine with putting up this facade and letting them believe this lie, but now my feelings have changed completely. My church family knows a little bit more about the situation than my friends, but there's still a lot they don't know, so I often get frustrated when they tell me to "stop being mean" to my mom when they don't know everything. They think they know the reasons behind my behavior, but there's a deeper explanation as to why I act the way I do towards my mother. They only see the surface of the problem, which is my mom being a helpless drug addict. However, they've never seen nor witnessed the verbal abuse, so it angers me when they automatically take her side without acknowledging my feelings!

For a while I was content with masking my pain for my friends and allowing others to believe whatever they like, but that is now a thing of the past. My feelings have completely changed, and I want them to know the true story. Not just because I'm always thought of as the bad guy, but because I think my friends (and other teenagers) will find comfort in realizing that we go through similar things and there are always brighter days ahead. More importantly, writing this book is *my* way of finding comfort in my own story as well. This book is my way of breaking free from my past and defying the odds that are against me in a way that people thought I would never be able to do.

I understand that my mother wasn't mentally herself while she was using drugs, but that didn't make it hurt any less. When she was calling me all those negative names, I didn't see a random drug addict. I saw my mother telling me how she really felt. The self-esteem issues that developed from this abuse lingered for many years even after I reached high school. Sometimes I still battle with low self-esteem to this day all because of her: my *mother*. Most people value their mother's opinion over anything else, and I used to be the same way until I realized that her opinion of me was untrue. It took some time, but I finally stopped believing the lies she had imbedded in me.

You can probably guess that I began to develop a hatred for my mother, and you would be absolutely right. In fact, I developed a *deep* hatred for her. After taking the verbal abuse for so long, I began to retaliate by treating her as horribly as she made me feel. Fighting fire with fire made me feel better about the situation, and I always justified my actions with "she deserves it." I didn't realize how bitter this whole ordeal was making me until I saw the effects of my angry behavior. I've dealt with insecurities, which ultimately caused me to develop a strong dislike for myself. It has also caused me to suffer from bullying, which led to a deep-seated internal anger that I took out on others. All those things were very difficult for me to overcome, but the hardest thing I've had to endure was caused by one of the people who was supposed to love me most: my mom. I know in this thing called life we're all going to have our fair share of pain and suffering, but this truly felt unfair.

Chapter 2

Child Protective Services

Our mothers are supposed to love and shield us from the dangers of the world as best as they possibly can, but mine was different. Instead of being my biggest protector, my mother became my own worst enemy. For as long as I can remember, I have yearned for my mother's love and acceptance. Instead of love, she gave me leftover bitterness and anger. Instead of accepting me, she rejected me and handed me over to child protective services. To make matters worse, when my grandparents attempted to gain custody of me, in an effort to give me a better life, she lied and said my grandfather molested me. To this day I wonder how a mother could inflict such an immense amount of pain onto her child.

I think that most, if not all, adults can agree that pain is a part of living. Well, my pain began shortly after I began living. I was only three years old when I was taken into custody of child protective services because of my mother's inability to care for me. While my mother did not have a physical disability, she did not have the mental capability to raise a child.

When I think about my mother giving me up, I struggle with forgiving her for this and all the countless horrible things she has done to me. It has been a challenge to overcome the abuse and mistreatment she has inflicted over these years. While some may not understand my pain when they realize that my mother never physically abused me, I want to remind everyone that not all abuse comes in the form of physical abuse. It is the emotional pain that can often hit the hardest.

Memories from my childhood still haunt me, like the time I was told to sleep on the floor when my grandparents had previously purchased a bed for my mother and I to sleep in. Instead, my mother and her boyfriend Tyrone ended up sleeping in the bed because, apparently, he had nowhere to stay. See, Tyrone was always first in my mom's world and everybody else came second to him — including me. Now, I understand that I was the product of a teen pregnancy (my mom got pregnant with me at the age of sixteen), and she was still very young and naïve. This could possibly explain her irrational behavior back then.

However, that does not negate the fact that time and time again she failed at taking proper care of me, and the examples are endless! For instance, besides sleeping on the floor, I can vividly remember hearing the constant arguments between my mother and Tyrone. It was almost like I was invisible, because they said things in front of me that a young girl should have never been exposed to. Whenever my mother and Tyrone disagreed on anything, it turned into a heated arguing match. They would yell at each other so intensely you would have thought they hated each other.

In hindsight, now that I really think about it, they more than likely did hate each other. Their relationship was extremely toxic, and it definitely had a traumatizing effect on me. I can remember crying very loudly while they were in the middle of an argument because I wanted them to stop yelling, but neither one of them stopped to see what was wrong with me. In fact, that happened many times. They would make up with each other and then start back arguing a few days later. It was a very vicious cycle.

My grandparents were never too far away and often tried to intervene as best they could. As you can probably guess, they didn't like Tyrone and they had every right not to. Tyrone disrespected my grandparents on several occasions, but my mother still stood by "her man." It absolutely disgusts me that my mother chose Tyrone over her own daughter and her parents when they told her he was no good. Not surprisingly, my grandparents were right about Tyrone. One day an argument erupted between my mother and Tyrone, but this time the argument permanently altered my life. This argument got so bad that a neighbor called the police and I ended up in custody of child protective services; this very moment still haunts me to this day.

In an ideal world this would have served as a wake-up call for my mother, causing her to leave him. She would have successfully regained custody of me, got cleaned up, and become a better parent. Unfortunately, that's the exact opposite of what happened.

I really wanted my mother and Tyrone to stop arguing. I often wished that we would become the picture-perfect family you see in the movies. Although Tyrone wasn't my father, I wanted them to get married and make me their main

7

priority. I ultimately wanted to experience having a perfect family like the other kids around me had. I desperately wanted my being taken away from my mother to motivate them both to change and become better people in order to do a better job at raising me. I was young, but I knew I didn't want a dysfunctional family. I wanted a close-knit family. A family where we build each other up, not tear each other to pieces!

To make matters more painful, I planned out what I wanted if my mother got completely fed up and finally left Tyrone. If it ended up being just me and my mom, I would have been completely OK with that. I always wanted an unbreakable mother-daughter bond, and to this day I still do. Thankfully, I've been blessed to have great women placed in my life to help fill that deep void. Sadly, there is a part of me that *still* remains unfulfilled.

I honestly just wanted to be loved in the way I saw other kids being loved. It felt like a pointless plan. I felt unimportant and I yearned for my mother's love, but I never received it. Unfortunately, that's probably what made me so bitter. I absolutely hated the fact that my mother stayed with Tyrone — the man who caused her daughter to be taken away. To this day it still hurts, because she was supposed to choose me! She was supposed to love me more than anything — especially him! She was supposed to shield me from the pain, not run around with the very person who caused the pain.

Shortly after the argument between my mother and Tyrone, I was taken into custody by child protective services. While I was there, I went through hell — literally. It happened during the springtime at the end of March shortly after my birthday. I remember the weather being warm but nothing like the sweltering heat we get during the summer months. I remember how there was a cool breeze in the air. I also remember this strange woman, who I later learned was a social worker, telling me to get into an unfamiliar car and put on my seat belt. I was very confused, but I was a very obedient child, so I did as I was told and got into the car.

Later, I had a thought that I probably should've ran as fast as I could from that car, but I didn't. Although I regretted not running away, I soon realized that either way I probably would've still ended up in the same predicament, no matter how much I resisted it. When the woman arrived at our destination, which I soon learned would be my new home, she asked me my name, and that's all I remember her saying to me before she took me into a room with other kids. All of the kids in the room looked lifeless. They appeared to be physically OK, but there wasn't any excitement behind their eyes.

I remember scanning the room in search of a child who was, well, a *child*. Yes, some of the kids were just as young as me but none of them possessed the joy and happiness children usually have, and I think it was at this very moment when I realized that this place was different and that I probably wasn't going home. After not finding anyone that I wanted to play with, I went and sat in a corner by myself, and that is exactly how I spent most of my time during the months that I was there — alone. Yes, they fed us, and we had beds to sleep on, however, this was nothing like what I was accustomed to. I was used to eating good meals in a nice warm bed, which is what most children are used to, but child services was different.

I specifically remember eating once and it was the worst meal I'd ever tasted to this day. Maybe it tasted so bad to me because I was disgusted with being there, but nonetheless it tasted horrible! I often skipped meals and refused to eat because of how terribly I was missing home. Most of the time the place was cold, which resulted in most of us kids having colds frequently. There was also a foul odor in the air the majority of the time. All of these things, combined with the fact that I was alone, caused me to develop problems that would continue well into my teenage years.

I was young, and I didn't know it then, but I was indeed depressed. Back then, all I knew was that I was sad and that I didn't like being there. Now that I know what depression is, I can see that I was going through a period of deep sadness. Almost every night I silently cried myself to sleep. That place sucked every bit of life out of me. I was no longer the happy child who always laughed and smiled. I had turned into a totally different person, and to this day I've never been quite the same. The experience with child services permanently altered my life, and to a certain degree I still haven't recovered — which is part of the reason why I began writing this book.

Although the majority of the time I was sad and lonely, there were some happy moments, but not because of the social workers or the other kids. The little happiness that I did have was when my grandparents came to visit. Most of the time when they visited, they noticed that I was losing weight very quickly. They would tell me, "Mya, you have to eat," but I wasn't trying to hear that at all. I had my mind set on not eating unless I was absolutely starving. Playing with my grandparents during those visits was the highlight of my little life back then. It was like for an hour or two I was in heaven, and I enjoyed every moment until they had to leave — then it was back to my normal routine of staying alone, keeping to myself, and not eating.

I stayed in child services' custody for nearly a year, but it felt like an eternity. Although I was just a little girl, I remember the experience so vividly, like it was yesterday.

Those months were by far the hardest thing I've ever had to endure in my life. I was taken away from the people I loved the most: my grandparents. Although they visited as frequently as their schedules allowed, I always wished I could simply leave and go home with them.

I think visits from them is what kept me sane, seeing as though some of the kids who were there with me had developed mental problems. I thank God I came out with no major mental issues but, as previously stated, this experience left me broken and bruised in various ways. To this day, I am still trying to make sense of it all and overcome the effects of my time in child protective services.

Chapter 3

The Custody Battle

Immediately after I was taken away, my grandparents announced that they wanted full custody of me. My grandparents visited as often as their schedules allowed, and visits from them were the only thing that kept my spirits high because they were my only source of happiness at that time. They were my hope, my joy, and most definitely my peace. Every time they visited, I wanted to leave with them, and each time I was told I couldn't my heart broke and I erupted in tears.

See, there is a reason why I wasn't allowed to leave with my grandparents, despite the fact that they were willing to take full custody of me. While I was in child protective services there was an all-out custody battle going on. For something to be considered a battle, there must be two opposing sides. Well, one side was my grandparents, of course, but the opposing side was my mother. Crazy, right? The battle for custody was exhausting and it seemed like all odds were against my grandparents. It was my grandparents who genuinely loved and cared for me versus my mother, who only wanted custody of me out of spite and to receive more government assistance.

You would think that the decision to give my grandparents custody was an easy decision for child services, but apparently it was not. My mother was well-prepared. She came to all of the court dates looking nice and she even had an attorney! It was at that moment we were all viciously reminded that people can and will use looks to deceive others. To my dismay, not only were my grandparents being opposed by my mother, but child services had joined in on the opposing side as well.

There was this one case worker, Cassandra, who stood out amongst the rest of the case workers, but not in a good way. Cassandra was persistent, to say the least. She was determined to make sure my grandparents never received custody of me. She even told them that they'd never see me again as long as she was living. Although Cassandra was persistent, my grandparents were also perseverant. Unfortunately, Cassandra was not the only obstacle my grandparents faced. My mother didn't just come to court looking nice; she put up a fight. Not only that, but she had a great attorney who came to win.

A couple months into the battle, in order to secure her win (I suppose), my mother decided to tell a devasting lie that would eventually backfire. She stood boldly in court and announced that my grandfather had molested me! Molestation is a serious matter, so you can probably figure out that child services definitely was not about to let me go home with my grandparents after such a shocking statement was made. As expected, child services had to follow protocol after this serious allegation had been made.

This allegation was shocking to my grandparents; they felt defeated, but they didn't give up. My grandparents kept fighting even though things got harder than they already were. Child services allowed my granddad to visit me, but the thing that was different about these visits was that somebody else was present in the room too. The other person in the room was a child services employee sent to study my behavior and interaction with my granddad.

After close examination and the studying of multiple visits, the employee came to the decision that my granddad had not molested me and that my mother was lying. I showed absolutely no signs of my granddad harming me. In fact, they noticed that my face lit up every time I saw him, which surprised child services since I was usually always looking sad and miserable.

Before the truth had even been revealed, my mother's attorney came up to my grandparents and said that he knew my mom was lying and that he was sorry, but he was simply doing his job. My granddad recalled that this almost completely fell apart when a meeting was called to discuss the accusations, but my mother failed to show. He had my grandmother, his pastor and few others with him to show solidarity and support. However, nothing could be done unless my mom came clean, and admitted that she had made it all up.

Hours went by as they waited for my mother. It was a painful period for my grandparents, and I'm sure the waiting was excruciating! My granddad's pastor became infuriated by the court's inability to see that my granddad was innocent and urged them to wait just a little longer to see if my mother would show. At what seemed like the moment the meeting would be called to an end, and the case to a close, my mother burst into the room!

She had a paper with everything written out that she wanted to tell the court. I suppose somebody helped her write it, but as she was about to read what was written, she stopped.

"I don't need to read this paper; I lied about everything," she confessed. "I only said my father molested Mya because my parents wouldn't let me do what I wanted to do."

"My boyfriend came up with the idea of accusing my father of molesting my daughter," she continued. "We just wanted to hurt them!"

After the truth had been revealed, my mother's argument became pretty much invalid. However, the battle was far from over after that. Not only did the court question my mother's credibility, but they also wondered if my granddad had forced her to recant her statement. To make matters even worse, more people attempted to gain custody of me. This thing had gone from a battle to becoming an all-out war!

My auntie and uncle began fighting my grandparents for custody of me. Sadly, I truly believe my auntie and uncle only wanted to gain custody in an effort to reap the monetary benefits of taking care of me. My aunt and uncle went head-to-head with each other, forgetting that my grandparents were still an unwavering part of the equation. It wasn't until the case had been placed in the hands of Judge White that things began to turn around. As previously stated, my grandparents were very perseverant, therefore they were at the courthouse every day, and early.

My grandparents both had jobs that they worked every day, but they still made time to come see about me and fight for custody of me. As previously mentioned, when Judge White became in charge of the case, things began to get better. No, when Judge White came into the picture, things took a turn for the best. One day in court, the judge was in a good mood. That day, I received the news I'd been wanting to hear. While in court, Judge White told my grandparents that he noticed how persistent they were and that he could tell they were amazing people.

After saying all of that, Judge White proceeded to say, in a joking manner, of course, that he was tired of seeing my grandparents every day and that he was granting them custody so that they could go home. After hearing that, my grandparents cried tears of joy and let out a sigh of relief. They could finally breathe now! It was all over — their baby was coming home! However, although they had gained custody in court, it took a few weeks for everything to be put into place and for papers to be signed before I could live with them.

After the process was complete, I came home on Thanksgiving Day in 2005, which was, and still is, by far the happiest day of my life. I could now finally reunite with my grandparents without worrying about them leaving me! I was extremely excited during the drive home. The social worker who drove me home was named Alicia, and her name is one I will forever remember too. When we parked in my grandparents' driveway, I hopped out of the car quickly, bursting with excitement. I gently grabbed Ms. Alicia's hand and pulled her to the back of the house before she could walk to the front door, while informing her that we didn't used the front door; we used the back door.

I knocked and when my granddad opened the door, I jumped into his arms quickly and cried tears of joy. I was finally home, and the fact that it was Thanksgiving made it even better, since I was starving because I refused to eat a lot while I was away. That day was and will forever remain the happiest day of my life!

I often wonder how my grandparents had the strength to endure such a difficult custody battle without giving up. When thinking about this, there are only two words that come to mind: faith and friendship.

Faith played a major role in my grandparents' steadfastness. While they were my source of hope, joy, and peace, their belief that God could do any and everything and that God could change any situation was their source of hope, joy, and peace. My grandparents were, and still are, devout Christians who love God very much, therefore I had no doubt that they believed with all their heart that "joy cometh in the morning" — and that gave them all the hope they needed.

Friendship was also a part of the reason why my grandparents didn't throw in the towel. My grandparents had some amazing friends rallying behind them, and one of them was our pastor. Our pastor prayed with my grandparents, came to court, and even came with my grandparents to visit a few times. My grandfather also had another amazing friend, Mr. Richard. Mr. Richard also prayed with my granddad. These are just two examples of the wonderful friends my grandparents had as their support system, but I'm sure there were many more.

Every day I think about how blessed I really am to have grandparents that stood resolute and were willing to gain custody of me. My grandparents are two of the strongest people I know. Without them, who knows where I would be?

Chapter 4

The Fakest Smile Ever

You know how in the beginning of this book I said that I'm not your average sixteen-year-old? Well, I've never been average at all. During my elementary and middle school years, I was probably weirder or stranger than I am now. As of matter of fact, I would say that the things I experienced in elementary and middle school shaped me into the person I am now. In elementary school I was shy and very scared of everything. It took a lot of courage for me to even have a conversation with someone. However, I eventually got used to my classmates, seeing as how I attended my elementary school from Pre-K all the way through fifth grade. The only thing I wasn't scared of was my academics, and I excelled in them.

In elementary school, I was picked on *a lot*. My glasses were thicker back then, and consequently I was constantly called *nerd* and *church girl*. At home I was taught that if someone is bothering you or picking on you, you stand up for yourself. Unfortunately, I was simply not in a state where

I could do so. Back then, I was overwhelmed with anxiety and I didn't have the courage to even think about standing up for myself. One rule of my household that I did adhere to though was never letting my peers see me cry. No matter how hurt my feelings were, I refused to cry in front of them, because not crying was my way of standing up to them. Not letting my peers get the satisfaction of seeing me cry was my way of winning. However, I definitely cried when I got home. In fact, there were many nights when I silently cried myself to sleep.

Even when I got home, I was careful to hide my tears. I'm sure my grandparents would've been understanding, but I was simply too timid to say anything. Furthermore, I feared that they would be mad at me for being weak and not standing up to others. Now that I look back on it, that probably wouldn't have happened, but back then I continued suffering in silence. Although I was internally struggling, I made sure that my grades were good, and this really took no effort at all. My academics always came naturally to me, and it is still like that today to a certain degree.

My peers taunted me all throughout elementary school, but each day I managed to walk into school with the fakest smile ever. They continually picked on me and I did nothing. I guess they assumed it didn't bother me because I always laughed everything off and acted like everything was OK. The truth was that I felt broken on the inside. However, I was really strong for my age, because I'd already experienced a lot of disappointments and internal struggles. In middle school things started out fine and I was happy because I thought things were finally getting better, but when I hit seventh grade things took a turn for the worse.

In seventh grade, I was faced with the constant taunting once again, but it was intensified. This time, the insults came from my own "friends." I don't think they even realized they were doing it. At the time, I was just happy to have a group of girls that I fit in with. In my mind it was normal for your friends to pick on you. However, my "friends" weren't the only ones who made me feel less than — my other peers did too.

In seventh grade, I reacted differently to the constant disrespect that resulted in me getting suspended. One day I was just not feeling good at all and I went over to my friend Brandy's table; she started playing with my hair, so I touched her hair. As a result, Brandy hit me! Unfortunately for her, I was already kind of not in a good mood. Normally, I would've laughed it off, because I always laughed it off whenever she hit me, but that day something came over me and I was infuriated. Before I knew it, I was throwing punches at her and we were fighting!

Everybody in the class was shocked because nobody was expecting me to stand up for myself. I even shocked myself because, honestly, I didn't know I had it in me. News of the altercation spread throughout the entire seventh grade and the big headline was that "Mya Joyce fought." Although it was nice to know that I won the fight, I was still disappointed in myself because that was my first time getting suspended. I got suspended for two days, but hey, at least I knew Brandy wouldn't even think about bothering me again.

Now that I look back on these moments, I realize that I reacted the way I did because these were emotions I'd been holding in for a long time. Everybody reacts to being bullied differently and although I got suspended, I'm thankful I didn't react in a worse way. For instance, too often we hear stories of young people committing suicide due to bullying. I know it sounds cliché but please, be mindful of how you treat others, and if you're a victim of bullying, tell someone if you can. If you just can't tell anyone, know that it is absolutely OK to defend or stand up for yourself.

Know that you are loved and always remember that you're important. People often attack others who are different, so find peace in knowing that being different is OK and that they're probably jealous of your individuality. Don't ever try to fit in, because you were born to stand out! Always walk with your head held high and take pride in yourself. I hope reading this chapter helps someone find peace in their situation, knowing that someone has experienced something similar. Finally, know this: if no one cares or understands, Mya does.

Now, if you are a bully it is imperative that you change. You would never want to be the reason someone decided to take their own life. Yes, you can change! I don't care who tells you any different, change is always possible. It's just a matter of you deciding that you will no longer add to the problem but be a part of the solution. Bullies are often dealing with something that has broken them so they, in turn, break others. There is a better way to express your emotions than stealing others' joy. You can try reading, writing, dancing, exercising, or something else, such as music. There are many positive outlets; you just have to find one that works for you.

Think about it; if you channeled all your anger and aggression into something positive, you would become a better person instead of tearing down someone else, which could potentially lead to you having to live with guilt for the rest of your life. I know firsthand how easy it can be to lash out at people or be mean towards people when you are faced with your own set of adversities in life, but you have to make up your mind that you won't let anger and bitterness overtake you. Take it from me, the reward of encouraging and inspiring people is much better than the temporary happiness you would get from seeing others as broken as you are.

Lastly, those who are trying to overcome being bullied, please don't turn into the predator. While you were being bullied you were the prey, but don't let your newfound confidence turn you into the predator who took that confidence from you. As you overcome, help others to overcome their struggles, because we are only as great as those around us. I hope this chapter encouraged someone because I got very emotional while writing this. If you don't take away anything else from this chapter, remember being different is OK, no matter what people say.

Chapter 5

Angry Black Girl

Speaking of emotions, black men and women are often stereotyped as angry individuals for simply expressing the way that we feel inside. I'm sure we've all seen the typical "angry black woman" in a movie or two, and I'm sure we all know a few in real life. I think all anger stems from hurt, and I'm speaking from experience. I've had people tell me I need to stop being angry with my mother, and honestly that caused me to become even more angry. When people tell me to just forgive and stop being angry towards my mother, I want to yell, "How could you possibly tell me to stop being angry when you don't even know the half of what she's done to me!" They don't see what goes on behind the scenes, so I feel as though they don't have a right to tell me that I should stop being angry.

I highly doubt that the average person's mother has ever told them that she wishes she aborted them. This is why I feel most people can't tell me to stop being so angry, because they really can't feel my pain. Yes, my mother told me that she wishes she would've aborted me. One day she came home high on drugs. My grandparents always told me not to open the door for anybody when I'm home alone — not even for her. She came and knocked on the door, and I went to see who it was without opening it. When I told her that I wasn't going to open the door because my grandparents told me not to, you would've thought I said the meanest thing in the world to her. She became enraged! That's when I knew that she was most likely high or drunk off something. Either way, it was painstakingly obvious that she wasn't sober.

She started going off about how I need to open the door because she's my mother and I should listen to her. She called me stupid, and then when she realized that I really wasn't going to open the door, she got even angrier and started saying the craziest stuff. However, the thing that hurt the most was when she said, "I should've aborted you."

Ever since that day I've never looked at her the same. I never viewed her as a mother, but there was always a piece of me that hoped she would leave the drugs alone and change her life around. Sadly, after that day, I no longer cared. When she said that, my preexisting hate for her dramatically increased. She probably doesn't even remember that day because she was so drunk or high, but I do, and I always will. I honestly think I handled that situation well; I've never told my grandparents about that day, because I knew they would be angry with her. As much hate as I felt toward her, deep down I knew she needed somebody to love her; my grandparents are the only two people in this world who truly love her. Honestly, I believe she deserves love, just not from me.

Every time I look at her, I think about all the stuff she's done to me. Unfortunately, we live together, so you can probably imagine how angry I get at times. I feel entitled to this anger, and you would never fully understand until you've experienced something like this. People say that she is human and that we all make mistakes. I agree that we all make mistakes, but some mistakes cost us more than others. Her mistakes came at the expense of losing her children. Yes, I said children. I am not my mother's only child; I have three other siblings. However, I don't think being human excuses being a bad mother! I'm not saying parents don't make mistakes, because they do. However, most parents don't become drug addicts and tell their children that they should've aborted them.

I also think that we should stop using the "everybody makes mistakes" excuse for bad behavior. Everybody does make mistakes, but we should all learn something from our mistakes. If we keep making the same mistake over and over, then it is no longer a mistake — it's a choice. My mother CHOSE drugs over her children over and over again. My mother CHOSE Tyrone over me. My mother CHOSE to participate in activities that would land her in jail. These were all her choices.

I'm sure the first one or even two times were mistakes, but after that she chose to do those things for herself, and I don't feel sorry for her at all. She's been clean many times, but after a few months or so she goes out and does drugs again. She continues to make bad choices even though she's had several opportunities to get herself together.

Forgiving and releasing anger isn't as easy as people make it seem, and I sometimes wish people would stop forcing it on me. I'm the child in this situation! I feel like they should be forcing her to give *me* an apology! I absolutely hate when people tell me I owe her a certain level of respect, because she owes me a certain level of respect as well. She hasn't given me the respect I deserve; therefore, I won't respect her either. She just doesn't deserve my respect, if we're being honest. She birthed me, so I'm supposed to give her the utmost respect? No, that's not how life works. I know most adults have the "that's your mother no matter what she does" mindset, but I don't!

I could sugar coat this part of my story, but I won't. I want to be brutally honest, because often adults have no idea how young people truly feel. Children suck it up, hold it in, and are fearful of releasing their true feelings because they feel like their words will just get beat back down their throat. I know I might sound bitter to some people, but right now I am more concerned with people understanding the effect that a drug-addicted parent has on a child. This is the result of years of pain, buried behind a painted-on smile and timid obedience.

Now, I refuse to suffer in silence! I believe by speaking out I can be healed, and one day I won't be as angry or angry at all. In the meantime, you don't get to just bring a child into the world and treat them like trash and call yourself a mother. Sorry, it just doesn't work that way anymore. You can't call your child every negative name in the world and expect them to just love you so much! I don't love her — if anything I hate her. I legit cannot stand her, and I'm tired of people trying to make me feel bad about the way I treat her.

Like I said before, she deserves every bit of this disrespect, and I'm going to continue to give it to her until *I'm* ready to stop. Call me mean, bitter, angry or whatever you'd like, but honestly, it's just the way I feel. Furthermore, I'm tired of people ignoring my feelings and defending her foolishness. Maybe I should have more compassion for her because she's mentally unstable, but honestly, I don't. I don't have any compassion for her because she's not as stupid or mentally unstable as people make her out to be.

For instance, if my mother can maintain friendships with normal people, then she's not *that* stupid. She just knows when to act stupid and when not to. I also feel like if she's able to maintain friendships, then she should be able to maintain or establish a relationship with her kids. She can talk on the phone with her friends all day and go out with them, but she can't even treat her kids right. How does that work? She's always choosing other stuff or other people, and at this point in my life, she's choosing her friends! She's made it perfectly clear that she doesn't care about me and my brother, so why should I care?

Other than the occasional birthday gift or Christmas gift, she does nothing for us. I guess she thinks that because she gives me a gift once or twice a year, I've forgotten about everything she's done. Well, I haven't, and I'm still salty about it. Yes, I'm angry, but I'm hurt too. Instead of just calling people angry, we should be empathetic, because we don't know the full story. My mentor once told me that depression is anger turned inward. This make a lot of sense because I can often get so angry it hurts.

I'm angry at my mother, and I refuse to allow people to make me feel bad about it. I'm allowing myself to feel and not just ignore the problem like I used to do. I understand that in order for me to heal, I can't ignore my feelings. I have to stop acting like the problem doesn't exist, because it does. I have to face my feelings and my trauma so that I can heal from it.

With this in mind, before you call me angry, know that I am simply hurt. Don't stereotype me, because although I am bitter and angry, I'm more than a stereotype. Maybe one day I'll be able to forgive my mother, and maybe one day I'll understand why she made the choices she made, but for now I'm allowing myself to feel, and right now I am angry.

Chapter 6

I Don't Want To Be Here

As previously stated, this book is my way of coming to terms with and living in my truth. Prior to writing this book, I hadn't faced my truth, but I managed to put it to the back of my mind and not think about it at all. I'd been living a lie for so long that I almost forgot who I really was. When I started writing this book, I quickly began reliving each and every moment.

As I wrote about each of my past experiences that negatively impacted me, it was like the emotions I felt in those very moments were coming back to me again. The anger, the hatred, the bitterness, the sadness, the anxiety, the depression — all of it. Each day was, and still is, a roller coaster. I often went through an array of emotions on a daily basis. Sometimes I would be happy, but only temporarily, because by the time night came around, I would cry myself to sleep. I sometimes even thought I was crazy because I could never for the life of me obtain and maintain true happiness.

Although I was internally fighting a battle every day, I was always careful not to show it. In my mind, crying meant I was weak, so even though I would cry myself to sleep at night, I was determined to not cry or show any sense of emotion in front of anybody else — friends and family included. In addition to not wanting to be viewed as weak, I felt like it was my duty to stay strong for my friends as well. I couldn't be the strong one of the group if I was crying and being caught up in my own emotions all the time. I was, and still am, the cheerful friend; the one who is always laughing and making others happy. As a result, crying at school is definitely abnormal for me.

For example, one day at school I walked in like I usually do, with gospel music blasting through my headphones because I always like to start my day on a positive note. I walked into school and went over to my group of friends and stood there with them. In the morning when I first get to school before the bell rings, I'm normally quiet because I like to mentally prepare myself before the day even starts. One of my friends noticed something about me was off and she asked what was wrong.

"I just don't want to be here," I said.

We both looked at each other and started laughing. *She* was probably laughing because she didn't want to be at school either, but *I* was laughing because I wasn't just talking about school. I was actually talking about life in general.

I really didn't want to live anymore, and I didn't want to be at school either. Therefore, my response definitely had a double meaning, but I wasn't about to let her know what I truly meant. After we finished laughing, I simply smiled at her and went back to mentally preparing myself for the day. Although I was determined not to show it, I wasn't in the best of moods because the night before I had a "moment." I found myself crying. Not just a regular cry, but the kind of cry you feel in your chest. I often cry when I get frustrated or angry, so I was crying but it was more out of anger instead of sadness. I do have moments of sadness, but last night was not one of those. It was pure anger.

You can probably guess who I got angry with — my mom, of course. Yes, I got so angry and upset to the point where I started to question my own existence. I started to think about how at peace I would be if I wasn't alive, so I decided that I just didn't want to be here anymore. I was convinced that death would be better than living my life, and I was hoping that I wouldn't wake up the next morning. I didn't attempt suicide, because I knew that would hurt my grandparents and that was the last thing I wanted, so I decided to just hope and pray that I miraculously wouldn't wake up in the morning, but I did. I woke up.

After the encounter with my friend, that next morning I began to think about different things throughout the day: my book (that you are now reading) and a specific scripture. When I started thinking about this book, I began to think about how before I started writing, my life was in pretty decent order. I had learned to cope with everything, and I mastered the art of not showing any emotion at all. I was basically numb to everything. I felt nothing. It seemed like once I started writing this book, all hell decided to break loose in my life.

It appeared as if bad things were happening every day, and I found myself becoming mentally and emotionally drained. I was tired of everything going wrong, and as a result, I thought about giving up on this book, because I thought it was causing too many issues. I wanted my happiness back, and I decided that giving up on writing the book would be the best way to do so. Although I so desperately wanted to be done with it all, something inside of me wouldn't let me be done with it. It was like I had to keep going because I knew I could help other teenagers and people just like me.

Besides my book, the other thing that kept crossing my mind was a specific scripture: "Give not that which is holy unto dogs, neither cast ye your pearls before swine..." Matthew 7:6 (KJV)

For the life of me, I couldn't understand why I kept thinking about this scripture. I spent all day trying to figure out what it meant, because there must have been a reason why I kept seeing it in my mind. I didn't get my answer, though, until I called Mrs. Holmes (she is a friend of the family, but you will read more about who she is later).

Mrs. Holmes told me that one application of the scripture is that we shouldn't waste our God-given gifts and talents on people who are unworthy, and then she asked me how it could possibly apply to my life. It didn't take me long to figure out that it meant that I should stop letting people get to me and stop letting people cause me to step out of my character.

The scripture might be minor to you, but honestly it was major to me. At this particular time, I realized that I had to get myself together — and by "get myself together" I mean adopt a better attitude and a better tolerance level. Getting myself together also means that while I know that people will try me, I can remain calm and collected when they do.

Along with these two thoughts, I realized that there must be a reason why I'm still here. I literally begged God to take my life away, but He didn't. Therefore, I concluded that there must be something greater for me and that I would eventually conquer my past. I still struggle with my emotions and it's been and will possibly continue to be an ongoing battle, but what I do know is that while it seems all hell is breaking loose, this book is helping me heal.

The day after having thoughts of suicide, just like any other day, I went from being happy to angry and from angry to sad. What I took away from my reflection on my book and the Bible scripture was that I'm progressing and getting better little by little, and that's all that matters. With that in mind, I ended that night on a positive note, knowing that it is OK to feel and be emotional. I was content and not crying as I had many times before, but I realized that tomorrow night I might cry again.

However, I also determined that it is absolutely OK to cry sometimes, because I'm still on this roller coaster called healing and I won't be completely healed overnight.

Chapter 7

You Are Not Alone

I told myself that by the time this book would be published, I would be in a better place. I wanted to be in a
better place mentally, emotionally, and spiritually. However, being in a better place has a double meaning in my life
sometimes. Sometimes I just want to be in a better place
in the sense that I don't want to be alive anymore. In fact,
I often get so emotionally and mentally messed up to the
point where I just believe everyone's life would be better if I
were no longer here.

These suicidal thoughts and feelings mostly stem from
guilt. I often blame myself for my mother's condition. See, my
mom gave birth to me when she was 16 years old. Therefore,
I ruined what should've been the best years of her life — her
teenage years. After having me, she decided to drop out of
school in an effort to take care of me. I ruined her chances at
receiving higher education and becoming something great in
life. This must be the reason she hates me! Honestly, I would
hate me too if I were her, because I basically ruined her life.

Although she sometimes abused drugs before she lost custody of me, my being taken away is what caused her to use drugs more consistently and become a full-blown addict. If I had never been born, none of this would have happened. Everything is my fault. I caused all of this!

This was my thought process, and it took me a very long time to change it. To this day, I struggle with feelings of guilt sometimes. It took a lot for me to realize that everything was not my fault and that everything that happened to my mother was a result of her own decisions. I had to come to terms with the fact that I didn't ask to be born into this world, but my parents both willingly made a choice, and here I am. Along with realizing that everything wasn't my fault, I had to realize that even though I've been through some difficult things in life, there's a reason why I was born and more importantly there *has* to be a reason why I'm still here.

Although I'm doing better mentally, suicidal thoughts have had a strong hold over me. For a while I thought I was crazy because, generally speaking, suicide is often looked down upon among black people. In other cultures, it is viewed as a very real problem. Unfortunately, many black people think suicide is a characteristic of other races and that it never happens in our community. However, this could not be further from the truth. Many black teenagers and black people in general have contemplated suicide, and countless black people have gone through with it.

I grew up in church and was taught that suicide is just as much of a sin as murder, but that doesn't stop the thoughts from coming to my mind. No matter how much I try, it seems like suicidal thoughts always come back to haunt me. Along with my belief that suicide is a sin, I never went through with it because of my grandparents. When I think back to the custody battle when my grandparents could've easily given up and thrown in the towel, it keeps me from giving up even though I so desperately want to.

I have often felt like I couldn't tell anyone around me because of the fact that "Christians just don't do those types of things" and I feared that I would be called crazy for feeling the way I did. Not telling anyone about these feelings and keeping them to myself only allowed them to fester.

If you're reading this book and you've experienced or are currently having suicidal thoughts, you are NOT crazy, and you are most certainly not alone. Many people have thought about suicide at least once — they're just afraid to speak about it. Suicide is very real, although it may not be commonly acknowledged. No, it is not an "other race thing" but it is an "everybody thing." With this in mind, don't think that what you're feeling is crazy, because it's not. However, you should strive to get better and if at all possible, seek help.

Seeking help doesn't always mean visiting a therapist or going to a counselor, but it could mean finding someone you trust and just opening up to them. Tell that person everything you're feeling! However, here's the key: it must be someone who is a great listener and/or can give you good, sound advice. I believe the person should push you to become greater. For example, if that person is just allowing you to stay the way you are, then you haven't found the right person. I say this because suicidal thoughts are no joke, and in order to overcome them, you need somebody who will help you get better instead of someone who allows you to mentally remain where you are.

Although seeking professional help is also looked down upon among black people, I believe that if you can get that kind of help, then by all means, you should go for it. I've tried professional help before. I went to a counselor and I was very optimistic about it. I really wanted to be free from this stronghold called suicidal ideations. However, I was hoping to receive a black counselor (no, I'm not racist; I just wanted somebody who could possibly relate to me more), but instead, I received a Caucasian woman. However, this didn't stop me from being optimistic about counseling.

I still went into the session with a positive attitude. I distinctly remember the counselor asking me one question.

"Why do you want counseling?" she asked.

I responded by giving her a basic summary of my life events, and at the end saying I wanted to be able to forgive my mother one day.

"Wow! I can't imagine going through anything like that," she said. "I've never been through anything."

It was this response that caused me to never want to attend another counseling session again.

About a month after attending that counseling session, I began to receive help in another form. I started talking to Mrs. Holmes (the wife of my granddad's friend). It was weird because originally, we were supposed to be talking about what law school is like. Mrs. Holmes is currently in law school and I want to be a lawyer someday. She originally offered academic advice, but somehow, I believed I could trust her. I began confiding in her and telling her everything that I'd previously been holding in for years. I even told her about the suicidal thoughts. She reassured me that I was not crazy and told me that more people have suicidal thoughts than you'd think. Mrs. Holmes and I still talk every day and confiding in her has had such a positive effect on my life. It's because of her that I was able to even write this book in the first place.

Mrs. Holmes is definitely a positive example of how talking to someone can help you recover from suicidal ideations. The counseling session serves as a bad experience with seeking help, but the journey to healing is a strange one and it goes differently for everyone. What worked for me may not work for you, and that is perfectly fine as long as we are all finding ways to overcome these thoughts. Just because counseling didn't work for me, it doesn't mean professional help won't work for you. Therefore, if you can, I think you should seek out professional help.

There are some great resources out there, and I encourage you to explore and find something that works for you and your journey. If you are unable to receive professional help, don't feel bad. Do what I, and many others, did. Find somebody who you can count on to be there for you and give you good advice. My person, Mrs. Holmes, is an adult. However, your person could easily be somebody your own age. As I previously stated, you have to find what works for you and your journey to healing.

Keep in mind that often suicidal thoughts don't just disappear overnight — especially if you're anything like me, because mine have been occurring for years. Don't beat yourself up if some days seem harder than others. Instead, embrace the fact that days are getting easier and that you're progressing.

Lastly and most importantly: if you are considering suicide, please don't go through with it. You are loved! If no one else loves you, God does, and I do too. Stay strong, you will overcome this, you got this! I'm rooting for you!

Chapter 8

I'm Not Supposed To Be Here

As mentioned in the previous chapter, suicidal thoughts had a strong hold on my life for a long time. Along with *wanting* to be dead, I believed I was *supposed* to be dead! You're probably reading this saying to yourself, "Um girl, what do you mean? Why would you think that?" Well, I believed this for a long time because I wasn't even supposed to be born in the first place. As a product of teenage pregnancy, I have concluded that I was definitely unplanned. In fact, I was a mistake.

All my life I'd been told, "God doesn't make mistakes." I have even told other people the same thing when they felt sad or suicidal, but I never fully believed it applied to my own life. People always told me that I'm special and that I'm here for a reason, but I was never able to wholeheartedly believe this because I wasn't even wanted in the first place! I never had a mother and father who were happy that their baby girl had finally entered the world. Instead, I had a mother who was young and naïve. A mother who had no clue about how to love and care for a baby because she was still pretty much a baby herself. I didn't have a father at the time either, because all he did was impregnate my mom and leave.

I always believed that my own mother not loving me was proof of the fact that I wasn't supposed to be here. In my mind, everybody else's mother loved them because they were meant to be alive. Sadly, mine didn't love me because I was supposed to be dead. While writing this book, I was in class one day and somebody said something that sent shock-waves through my body.

"Mothers automatically love their children unconditionally as soon as the child is born," one of my classmates said.

After hearing this, I immediately broke down crying because *my* mother didn't love me. To me, this was yet another sign that I shouldn't have been born. As usual, nobody even noticed my tears until the teacher asked me what was wrong.

"I don't feel good," I said, giving my usual response when someone would catch me crying at school.

When I would often lie about what was really wrong with me, people were usually convinced by this answer, so it quickly became my go-to response to avoid sharing my feelings with anybody else.

Another reason I believed I should have been dead was because when I was very young, around three to four months old, my grandparents and I were in a car accident. One day we were coming home from church and it was raining very hard, so the roads were slippery. Long story short, the car hydro-planed, and we ran off the road. We walked away from the accident with just a few scratches, but we went to the hospital anyway. The doctor was confused as to how I made it out alive, because apparently the seat belt in my car seat had come off! I somehow got out of the car seat, which should have resulted in me dying or coming close to it, but all I had was a few scratches.

For the life of me, I could not understand why I was still living. I couldn't understand why God wouldn't just go ahead and take my life away already! Some days, while writing this book, I would be in such emotional turmoil to the point where all I could do was cry! I desperately wished to stop existing, even for just one moment. There were days when I wanted to just stay in bed all day and sleep my life away. There were nights when I cried myself to sleep hoping that I didn't wake up in the morning.

Each time I would wake up it seemed like someone had pressed an imaginary "repeat" button in my life, and the vicious cycle would start all over again. This cycle continued for a while. Those days and nights still come, but I've finally realized that *I actually am supposed to be here!* I believe that my purpose is to help people that have experienced something similar to my own story, and even those who have experienced something completely different. It took me a while to come to this realization, but at least I came to it at last.

Along with realizing that I have a purpose, I realized that my still being here after all the bad things that have happened to me must mean something. Yes, me being conceived was a mistake, but me entering this world was most certainly not! There's a reason why God didn't allow my mother to miscarry with me or abort me. There's a reason why even though I came close to death, I didn't die. Remembering this thought alone is what got me through some of my roughest times. Even though I had come to this realization, I still had some low moments. However, when I was at my lowest and I started to contemplate suicide all over again, the simple thought of "if God wanted you dead, you would be dead, but you aren't" would help me to calm down.

Coming to this realization was surely a process and it was as if I was fighting a mental battle every day. Most of the struggles we face stem from mental battles, and I can attest to this. I had genuinely believed that I was supposed to be dead for years, and I acted and thought accordingly. Thankfully, changing my way of thinking meant I had to change my entire life.

Well-meaning people try to tell you to get over any negative feelings, emotions, or thoughts, but they never tell you *how* to get over them. They make it seem so simple, but honestly, it's easier said than done. They never tell you what going through the process feels like, and that's where I come in. I hope telling my truth can help others in their healing process, because that is part of the reason why I even decided to write this book.

For me, some days I would wake up happy and have the best day ever. Recently, I woke up happy. I prayed and started my day. The key to me remaining happy that day was the fact that nobody said anything to trigger my emotions. As long as I remained untriggered, my day continued to run smoothly. The problem is that my happiness depended on other people, and sometimes this is still the case.

There are days when I would wake up feeling very sad and depressed. Nobody had to say or do anything specifically, but I would wake up feeling miserable. For example, one morning I woke up feeling down. I even cried that morning and I *never* cry in the morning before school. I usually only cry at night when I'm sure no one can hear or see me. On this particular morning, I was an emotional wreck and I felt crazy because the previous day had been good. When I got home, once again the thought of me being a mistake entered my mind, but I started to write, and I immediately felt better. Writing is my outlet and I encourage you to find yours as well, because it can really help you channel those emotions into something positive instead of just making you a bitter, angry person.

As you can see, there were good days and bad days. However, there were those "in between" days as well. On the "in between" days, I would wake up happy or sad and then as the day progressed, my feelings would change and become the complete opposite. A good example of one of my "in between" days would be one morning when I woke up completely tired and worn out — more so mentally than physically. I had reached the point where I was just mentally and emotionally burned out. That morning was really weird. I went to school and was physically present, but mentally I was elsewhere. However, my day turned around and I gained a sense of happiness after a little over half the day had passed. As I said before, it's like I'm living a double life because nobody at school has any idea of what I've been through. I often feel like I have to remain happy and cheerful throughout the day in an effort to keep others from seeing how depressed I am. I must admit, sometimes acting happy does help me gain a sense of joy. I suppose the saying "fake it until you make it" might have some truth to it.

Chapter 9

Daddy Issues

I n previous chapters, I mentioned my mom's boyfriend, Tyrone. Well, in case you were wondering, Tyrone is *not* my dad. I really don't know where my dad was during all of the things that happened to me, such as the custody battle. It is likely that he probably doesn't even know about everything that happened, but the one thing he does know is that my mom is mentally unstable, which led to me being placed in my grandparents' custody. However, I don't know where my dad was during all of the mess, because I didn't find out who my father was until I was a little over eight years old.

One day, not too much longer after I turned eight, my grandmother took me to a mental health place that was also like a community health center. When I was younger, I was terrified of any place that had to do with health and checkups simply because I hated shots and vaccinations (I still hate them to this day). I was very intelligent for my age and I was able to put two and two together very quickly. Upon arriving at this place, I had already read the name of the building and

I had heard adults talking about this place before (yes, I was a nosey child). When I heard adults talking about it, they basically said the health center was a place for people with mental problems, individuals who want birth control, and people who want to know who their fathers are.

As previously stated, when I was younger, I was very smart, so I was sure I wasn't there because I had mental problems. Although at first it did cross my mind because my mom has mental problems. As a result, I thought maybe somehow her mental problems rubbed off on me! I quickly denied this thought because I was doing well in school, and there was no way I had mental issues.

"Is it possible that my grandparents brought me here for birth control?" I asked myself.

Now, I knew good and well that there was absolutely no way I was there for birth control, so I quickly tossed that thought to the side! At that point in my life, I didn't even know how babies were made, let alone think about sex. After getting rid of the first two options of mental health and birth control, I began to ponder the third and final one — finding out who my father was. I realized that the third option wasn't too far-fetched, and I decided to ask my grandma.

"Am I here to find out who my father is?" I asked.

My grandmother confirmed my suspicion. Soon after being told why I was there, I realized that some type of testing had to be done in order for them to find my biological dad. After coming to this realization, I began to cry hysterically. I was scared of needles and I had heard — from adults, of course — that when people get DNA testing, they have to get blood drawn.

By the time we made it in the building, I was crying uncontrollably. I was still afraid because I honestly hated needles and the thought of them made me tremble. Yes, I was a little dramatic, but needles just do something to me. Anyway, we sat in the waiting area until my last name was called. When it was my turn, someone took me into the back and sat me in a room. While waiting for the person to come administer the test, I was a nervous wreck. The funny thing is, I was so worried about a needle that I completely forgot why I was really there!

Finally, the person administering the test walked in.

"What's wrong?" she asked with a concerned look on her face.

I was still crying.

"You're about to stick a needle in me," I said with a whimper.

To my dismay, she started laughing at me! In my head I was thinking, *"Is she crazy? Why is she laughing? This is not a laughing matter!"* I guess she realized I was looking at her like she was crazy, because after a few seconds of me just staring at her she spoke up.

"Oh, honey! I'm not sticking a needle in you. I'll only be taking a sample of your saliva," she said.

Boy, was I relieved after she said that! I stopped crying immediately and turned my frown into my usual smile. After hearing this great news, I was ready to take the test. She took a sample of my saliva and told my grandmother that she should receive the results in the mail soon.

We did receive the results in the mail a few weeks later. The test confirmed who my father was. Upon hearing the news, I was a little conflicted because one part of me was happy that I finally knew who my father was, and the other part of me was scared to meet and get to know somebody new. Most little girls would've probably been glad to meet their father, and I was happy about it — but only to a certain extent. I didn't really care to get to know somebody new because as far as I was concerned, my granddad was my father. My granddad was the one who had taken care of me for practically my entire life. I didn't know it back then but now as I look back on it, I realize that I was trying to guard my heart from experiencing more hurt. However, I didn't see it that way at the time.

Despite my thoughts, I ended up meeting my father anyway. One day he came to our house to meet me for the first time and it was very awkward. We sat and talked — actually, we sat and *he* talked while I just nodded my head. He mostly just asked me questions about myself and my likes and dislikes. When I was younger, I had terrible anxiety and very low self-esteem to the point where I was terrified to even look people in their eyes when talking to them. At that point in my life, I wasn't really feeling the "meet and get to know new people" thing, and the only people I really knew were my grandparents and my brother.

However, I tried to force myself to interact with my dad, but I just couldn't. It's hard to explain, but I was too scared to even talk to him, therefore I only said what was necessary like "yes" and "no" when he asked me something. He seemed really interested in me though, which is why my opinion about having him in my life changed. He seemed genuinely interested in me, so I decided to give him a chance. That night after he left, I got excited at the thought of having my father in my life and building a bond with him. Both of my best friends at that time had their fathers in their lives, and I was really happy that I finally had a chance to experience that for myself.

Unfortunately, the excitement quickly died down. The bond that I was so happy to be building wasn't happening at all. After he came to see me that day, I expected to see him again very soon, but instead, I didn't see him for months!

This taught me to never get my hopes up, because even if something good does happen, it's not going to last. I wondered why he even came to the house in the first place if he wasn't going to stay around? I would've preferred for him to not come around at all than make appearances during Christmas and invite me on a summer trip occasionally.

Today, my relationship with my dad is very much still the same. I'll admit, he has done some nice things for me like the time he threw me a birthday party at his mom's house when I turned nine, but to be honest, I *still* don't know him. Nowadays, my father thinks that it's my responsibility to maintain our relationship and I completely disagree. For example, one day he texted me and asked why I don't I call him and talk to him more, and I was completely taken aback because I didn't know that it was *my* responsibility to call and check up on a *grown* man who seems to not want to talk to me! Yes, he pays my phone bill every month, but that's about it. We don't talk that often and when we do it seems like we always argue. The "arguments" are really just me telling my dad how I feel and him getting offended by it.

One time I asked him for 50 dollars to pay dues for Beta Club at school. Although he is my father, I never like asking him for anything. I only asked him because my grandparents just did not have the money at the time, so I texted him and asked him for the money and he brought it to my house. Shortly after that, I texted him a "thank you" even though I told him thank you in person when he brought the money. To my disappointment, this man didn't even say "you're welcome." He just took the opportunity to ask me why I don't come around and call him more. After he asked that question, I decided to tell him how I really felt.

"I feel like you don't really care about me," I texted him. "You spend time with your other kids all the time and I feel as though since you are the adult, you should be the one reaching out to me, because I am the child!"

"You're being disrespectful," he replied. This really got my blood boiling!

"You don't realize how all this has affected me. You're trying to dismiss my feelings!"

I even told him I was crying, and he still didn't care. I could tell he didn't care because instead of acknowledging my feelings, he chose to dismiss me. Honestly, I was surprised by his response to me telling him how I felt.

"Mya, I give you money and I pay your phone bill! You should be the one to reach out to me and come to my house!"

"That's fine, we don't have to talk then," I said, ending the conversation.

I was texting paragraphs to him, and he was only responding by chastising me for being disrespectful! I was done! I felt, and still do feel, like if he really wanted to be in my life, then he would call and check on me and come to *my* house. I believe that if someone really wants to be in your life, then they'll definitely make it known. I feel as if he wants me to chase him — a full-grown man! I refuse to do that! After voicing my opinion and also mentioning how he treats his other kids and makes time for them, he decided to snap back at me.

Now, after hearing this, I was really taken aback because I'm a child and he's my father. I appreciate everything he's done for me, but I'd much rather him not give me anything than to have him buy me things only to throw it back in my face whenever I voice my feelings! To me it's really weird, because a father is supposed to take care of their children financially, and my grandparents have done this my entire life. My grandparents have spent much more money on me than he has. It amazes me how he thinks 50 dollars here and there makes him a good father, when it doesn't! As previously stated, I appreciate everything he's done for me, but what he fails to realize is that material things will never be more important than time.

Yes, he's given me money, but what about the time when I literally poured my heart out to him? I told him everything I was feeling and everything I've ever felt towards him. I told him about how I used to cry because I thought that something was wrong with me and that maybe that was the reason he didn't want me. I kept it all the way real with him, and instead of taking responsibility for his actions, he flipped the situation around on me as he always does. My dad has a way of making it seem like everything is my fault. Apparently, it was my fault we didn't have a good relationship, and it was my fault we never spent time with each other. This ordeal occurred about a year ago, and ever since then I've looked at him differently.

I'd much rather not talk to him at all than for us to talk occasionally and end up arguing about the same thing every single time. Sadly, I know I'll never get through to him. Sometimes I wish that I would've never met my father, because it seemed as if my life was perfectly fine before I met him. It seems as if he just brings another set of problems into my life, because some of my low self-esteem and depression stems from him. There's a lot more I could say about my father, but because I have a certain level of respect for him, I won't say more. However, I hope that if he decides to read this book that he finally realizes how much he's affected me over the years.

I went through periods of questioning my own self-worth because I thought that if my own father didn't like me, then there must be something wrong with me. I spent many years trying to figure out what that "something" is, but I have yet to figure it out. At first, I thought that maybe it's because he doesn't know how to love a little girl because the rest of his children are boys. I quickly invalidated this thought, though. My father and his girlfriend, Tee, have been together for thirteen years. Her daughter was around five when they got together, so he pretty much raised her as his own.

My dad treats his girlfriend's daughter like I've always wanted him to treat me. No, I'm not jealous. I just sometimes wish I could have that side of my dad, because he treats her so good, you'd think she was his biological daughter. I have nothing against Tee and her daughter, who is now in college; I love them. This lets me know that my feelings are not coming from a place of jealousy, but more from a place of wishing I had a bond with my father.

For many years, I often wondered why he didn't love me like he loved his girlfriend's daughter. She could've been the sister I always wanted, but he never really paid much attention to me. He loved her very much though, and I admire how good of a father he is to her. It's a beautiful thing, and I wish I could say the same about our relationship. Sometimes I still wonder what I lack or why I'm not lovable, but I have to remind myself that I lack nothing and that I am worthy of being loved the correct way.

I think after reading this, my dad will understand me better. There's a lot more to Mya than he, and everybody else, realizes. For example, the most significant thing that happened to him in 2005 was probably him getting together with Tee. However, the most significant thing that happened in 2005 for me was being able to come home. He doesn't even know about the custody battle. With that being said, this chapter may ruffle a few feathers with him, but this is just me telling *my* story and only hoping that he'll read this and realize that it wasn't written to attack him. My dad has done some nice things for me. I hope he takes heed to some of the things I've said and that he and I can learn more about each other and have a better relationship in the future.

Chapter 10

The Purpose In My Pain

In addition to family, church has always been an important part of my life. Ever since I can remember, I've gone to church every Sunday and Wednesday, and when I eventually joined the choir, Thursdays as well. Sometimes church is viewed as this serious place where you can't be yourself, but that's not true at all. Church *is* a serious place because it's a place of worship, but you are definitely allowed to be yourself. One time when I was around eleven or twelve years old, I was in church on Sunday and everybody was shouting.

Just in case you don't know what shouting is, it's not yelling, but it's a form of praising God. Shouting is basically dancing for Jesus and giving praise unto Him. That Sunday everybody was shouting, and then there was me. I was sitting down staring into space, because I was honestly ready to go home at that point and it seemed like they were never going to stop dancing. Whenever everybody got calm, somebody started shouting again and boom! The cycle continued. I was getting fed up! I was sitting there minding my business when one of the older girls, who I consider a big sister, came and got me.

She took me to the front of the church where everybody was shouting. We walked in a circle three times and on the third time, I was just ready to go. Suddenly, I felt something, and I started shouting too! I can't really put into words what the Spirit feels like, but when it touches you, you know exactly what it is. After I shouted, I started crying and the ushers brought me tissue. Afterwards, I was mad because I thought I made myself look crazy! I told myself that I was going to go join a mosque because I don't think Muslims shout. I was dead serious.

I was mad because I allowed myself to be crazy. Back then I thought shouting was weird and I always told myself that no matter how hard life got, I'd never shout because there were other ways to show God how thankful I was without making myself look strange. That was my logic back then. Now I see nothing wrong with shouting. However, is it something I'd personally do every Sunday? Goodness, no! I only shout when I feel led to — if that makes sense. On the other hand, a person can shout every Sunday and not really live a godly life, therefore I don't believe shouting determines where you stand with God.

When I was younger, I believed strongly in God and I honestly loved Him. I prayed daily and would even read the Bible. I remember being ten years old and literally crying out to God to heal my mother. However, as I got older my love for and belief in God began to fade. I suppose my belief in God weakened because it didn't seem like He heard my prayers. Everybody else was receiving blessings from God and He was answering their prayers, but for the life of me, I couldn't figure out why He wouldn't answer mine. By the time I turned fifteen, my faith in and love for God was almost completely gone. I'd told myself that He didn't like me, but He loved everybody else. Therefore, I still talked about God while not even believing the words that were coming out of my own mouth.

In addition to losing faith, I was also no longer shy in church. I developed relationships with some of the church members and church was no longer boring for me. I began to enjoy it. Singing in the choir became fun, and church eventually became one of the only places that took my mind off the pain that I was experiencing. Now, even though my faith in and love for God was slipping, I still participated in church. In fact, I'd say I participated in church even more after my faith took a hit. Church became more of like a social place for me rather than a spiritual place. I'm a prime example of how you can sit in church every Sunday and hear the pastor, but not really *hear* anything. I've sat in church some Sundays (and Wednesdays) and let my mind wander everywhere. However, thankfully there were some Sundays when I would sit and pay attention and learn a thing or two from the sermon.

I know most teenagers consider church to be a boring place, but that isn't the case with me. I love church, but I don't have a strong relationship with God to show for it. I even went through a season where I did the "forbidden thing" — questioning God. I wanted to know why God was allowing me to continue living in such unhappiness. I even questioned His reason for still having me on this Earth. At one point, I was ready to leave the world. I was doing a very good job at hiding this because every Sunday, Wednesday, and Thursday, I went to church smiling and spreading joy. I was doing such a good job at acting that some of the people from my church will probably be shocked when reading this chapter.

At school, I was even still being viewed as the "church girl." I still talked to my friends about God and posted the "churchy" quotes — the whole nine yards. I even stepped in and defended church when my peers stated that they thought church people were too judgmental. You would think I was madly in love with God, but that was just not the truth. Now, I still acknowledged God was *God*, but I didn't believe He had plans to "prosper me" or give me an "expected end" like the Bible says.

After meeting my mama (not my biological mother, but Mrs. Holmes), she persuaded me to develop a relationship with God for myself. Eventually she succeeded, but at first, I was just not trying to hear it. Slowly, I realized that maybe, just maybe, God didn't dislike me. Coming to this realization was definitely a process because I still couldn't understand why God wouldn't change my mother and why He would want me to experience all the pain that I'd gone through. My mama explained that a person has to want change for themselves and that God doesn't force anything on anyone.

Basically, my biological mother isn't going to get better until she's ready and nobody, not even God, was going to force her to change. Realizing this truth was quite painful, but it was the first step on my journey to building a better, stronger relationship with God.

Nonetheless, church has always held a special place in my heart. I've practically grown up in church, and as a result my church family is my second family. I've developed great relationships with some amazing people. My pastor and his wife have always been supportive. I know I can go to them if I ever need to talk and they'll never steer me wrong. Here's a fun fact about my church: the same day I was released from child protective services (Thanksgiving 2005) is the day we got a new church building.

My church family is composed of some of the sweetest, most amazing people. However, there have been times when they've corrected me about my interactions with my mother but didn't consider my feelings. For example, one time one of the church members heard me calling my mother by her first name and she scolded me.

"You shouldn't call her by her first name," the woman said. "You're supposed to call her 'mama.'"

What this person didn't know, and probably still doesn't know, is that I've never called my mother "mom" or "mama." Her first name is the only thing I've ever called her because she's never been a mother to me. I don't know her as "mama"; I know her as her first name. Now, I understand that the person from church probably doesn't know my full story. She only sees me calling my poor, helpless mother by her first name, which is normally considered disrespectful. However, I kind of think that she should've put two and two together and figured out that there was obviously a reason why I call my mother by her first name.

Nonetheless, I have no hard feelings towards the well-meaning church member, because I don't think she meant any harm. She isn't the only person at my church who doesn't know my story. In fact, I don't think anybody, except my pastor and his wife, knows what happened. Of course, they know I live with my grandparents, but they don't know *why* I live with them or *when* I started living with them. They know my mother is a drug addict and that she's mentally unstable. I am sure they see me being mean and rude to my mother sometimes, but they don't see when she's mean and rude to me! I don't blame them for trying to correct me, because they really do think they know everything that happened, but after reading this book they'll finally know my story — my *whole* story.

All in all, I love my church and I thank them for supporting and loving me the way they do — which is why I will always defend church as a whole when my peers say things like "church people judge too much" or "church people always act holier-than-thou." All churches and Christians are not the same, and there will always be one rotten apple who judges and criticizes people. However, I don't think we should let those few bad apples stop us from going to church.

God (and church) is what gave my grandparents hope during the custody battle. My pastor and his wife were all there for my grandparents, which is another reason why I will forever be grateful for them. Church is supposed to be a place of love and joy, so if you're not feeling that love and joy, then maybe you just haven't found the church for you. However, please don't label believers as a whole as judgmental. If you are receiving that love, then don't let that one person deter you from receiving the much-needed love that you get from church.

I urge teenagers not to feel pressured to have a perfect relationship with God, because it takes time. Adults sometimes expect us to be as far along into God as they are, and sometimes that's simply impossible. It often seems like they expect us to be perfect, and that's not going to happen. If you're a teenager wanting or trying to develop a relationship with God, try to just focus on bettering yourself and not focusing on the strict expectations adults can sometimes place on us. This rule could really be applied to every area of life: focus on yourself and not other's expectations and you'll be fine. God sees your effort and He loves you so much!

Personally, I struggled with living up to the expectations of certain adults. For a long time, I thought a relationship with God meant you had to be perfect. I thought that since I knew I would never be perfect, then I shouldn't even bother trying to have a relationship with God. It took a lot of talking but my mama (Mrs. Holmes) eventually got me to realize that a relationship with God isn't about being perfect, but it's about becoming a better person and getting to know God for yourself. When I accepted this, it became a lot easier for me to develop a relationship with Him.

My relationship with God is still, to this day, a work in progress. Day by day, I'm regaining my faith in Him. I've realized that the pain I experienced was not Him punishing me, but Him preparing me. In the words of my mama, He's "grooming [me] for greatness" and I'm excited to develop a relationship with God for myself. There's purpose in my pain, and I'm finally ready to find out what exactly that purpose is.

Chapter 11

Let's Talk About Sex

O ne of the things church has taught me is that there is always a spiritual side to things. One of the spiritual aspects of what I have gone through with my mom is that I am confident that I have to break the generational curse of teen pregnancy and drug addiction in my family. In every generation of my family, at least one person had a baby while they were still a teenager. For many years I feared that this curse will be passed on to me. I'm still a virgin, but for some reason I still have a very strong fear of becoming a teen mom. My mother was one of the teen moms of her generation, and I fear that I'll end up just like her. I suppose this fear is kind of healthy because it's one of the reasons why I refuse to have sex.

Teen pregnancy is not only a problem in my immediate family, but it's a problem throughout my generation as a whole. I think teen pregnancy shouldn't be such a taboo subject because it's something that a lot of young people need to hear about. Adults tend to just tell us to not get pregnant, but they never really go into depth. I'm the type of person who, if you just give me the bare minimum information, I'll go and do my own research and I'll continue searching until I feel content with the amount of information I've learned. That need to research information may come in handy in certain situations, like when I have a school assignment, for example, but curiosity sometimes does more harm than good.

For instance, I never really got the "sex talk" and I'm sure I'm not the only teenager who hasn't. I was only told not to do it because I'd end up pregnant, and that was the end of it. However, being the curious person that I am, I was not content with that small amount of information. I went to my good "friend" — the internet — and found some interesting things, to say the least. Adults weren't talking to me about sex, but the internet had a lot to say! Whew chile, let's just say I didn't know what sex really was before! After "researching" for a few hours, I knew exactly what sex was, how to do it, and how it feels. Not to mention I saw some things that I shouldn't have seen in the process.

I know I'm not the only teenager who can be very curious at times, and I'm sure we all have heard the saying "curiosity killed the cat." With that said, adults should be more informative. I'm not saying adults should go into graphic details, but a little more information would be helpful, such as talking about STDs and using protection. I was very lucky because I went to the internet to get a better understanding, but imagine if I had gone to a boy with the questions I had! You probably know exactly what would have happened. I think teenage pregnancy is a result of curiosity raging in teens, combined with adults' tendency to treat sex as a taboo subject. Due to our curiosity, we sometimes learn by trial and error, resulting in teen pregnancy and contracting STDs as well.

Teen pregnancy is a very serious matter, and I think it could be avoided in many cases if we simply talked about it. If we took away the negative connotation when talking about sex and had informative conversations about it, then there would be no reason for us to have to experience sex by trial and error. We wouldn't have to go out and experiment, but even if some decided to still try sex for themselves, they would at least know to be safe and use protection.

Adults around us aren't having serious conversations with us about sex. Consequently, we are being taught by the internet, pop culture, and our friends. It seems as if pop culture these days promotes sex. By learning from pop culture, we soon begin to believe that sex is almost inevitable, which in turn makes us not care, so we go ahead and do it anyway. Pop culture doesn't tell us about what could possibly happen after having sex, though. When we go to our friends who've already had sex, they normally encourage us to go ahead with it. We're essentially teaching ourselves about sex, which is why when we ask questions, adults should answer them instead of looking down on us or judging us.

I'm a product of teen pregnancy and the saying "babies shouldn't be raising babies" is definitely true. I'm not saying every teen mom will turn out like my mother, but they often do. My grandparents are devout Christians and I know they never talked to their children about sex. They only gave the "*don't do it*" and that was it. My mother's friends had a very strong influence on her and they were participating in sexual activities, so she thought she could do it too without anything happening. My mother is a great example of trial and error — she tried having sex, but unlike her friends, she got pregnant. After getting pregnant with me, my mother's life practically went downhill.

My mother is just one example of a teen mom and there are countless other examples — some of which turned out to be very successful. Although some teen mothers turn out OK, some don't. The ones that were successful had to struggle before things got better. My point is this: I urge all teenagers to ask questions, get clarification on things you don't understand, and don't experiment out of curiosity. STDs and teen pregnancy are very real consequences of experimenting, and this can definitely happen to you no matter how much you believe it can't.

Sex is a very sacred thing that was ideally created for married people, which is why adults often encourage us not to do it. Think about it: sex is for adults and sometimes even grown people can't handle it. Soul ties are also very real; therefore, I encourage teenagers everywhere to think twice before you "experiment." Ask yourself if you really want to be spiritually and emotionally connected to that person for the rest of your life, even if you do part ways with the person. More importantly, you should ask yourself if you are willing to risk having to bring another life into the world so soon, and are you willing to risk contracting any type of STD.

Another thing I want to address for teenagers is oral sex — it is considered sex too! Your friends might make it seem like it's not really *sex,* sex because there's no penetration occurring, but it's definitely sex. You can't get pregnant (or get someone else pregnant) from oral sex, but you sure can develop soul ties and contract STDs from it! You might tell yourself that you won't get pregnant or that you won't get an STD, but those two things can happen to anybody. For this very reason, I suggest refraining from all sexual activities, which can be very hard at times, because as a teenager your body is changing, your hormones are raging, and that makes it even harder to resist the temptation. With that said, stay strong, because good things always come to those who wait, and this can be applied to all other areas of life as well.

To the teenagers who've already done the deed, you are not "damaged" or "nasty" or whatever else people tend to call it. You simply allowed your hormones to take over, and it is completely normal for your body to want to have sex. Your life isn't over. In fact, this can be a new beginning for you. You may have already lost your virginity, but you can always turn to celibacy. However, if you insist on having sex, just make sure you're using protection, because you never know if your partner has an STD and you don't want to get pregnant (or get somebody else pregnant). You should keep in mind that all protection is not 100 percent effective. Most condoms are 98 percent effective (if used correctly) and you could very well end up being a part of the 2 percent that gets pregnant or contracts a disease.

While we're on the subject of pregnancy, let me tell you my story about it. No, I've never been pregnant; I haven't even had sex before. However, since I was little, I knew that one day I wanted to carry two children of my own and I still do feel like this today. I want to give the love that I so desperately wanted, but never received. I also want to have someone who'll always love me no matter what, and I know my children will do that. I never want to be alone, and I know with my own children, I'll never be alone. Sometimes I even thought about what life would be like if I decided to have kids right now, but I always push those thoughts aside REAL quick because, no. Just no.

My grandparents fear that I'll be like my mother, so I'd never want to give them another headache. Having children right now would not only affect my life, but my grandparents' lives as well. I simply can't afford to risk that right now.

I think the loneliness I'm feeling will all be worth it in a few years or even a year from now when I'm in a better place. I've made up my mind that no matter how lonely or sad I get, I'll wait until I'm married and well-established in my career to have children.

Part of the reason for writing about this topic is because I wish sex had been explained to me in much more detail. My goal is for this chapter to serve two purposes: to help other teenagers who, like me, aren't getting real conversations about sex, and to give adults an idea of what to say instead of the *"just don't do it."*

Chapter 12

Failure Is Not An Option

Like church, school has always been an important part of my life. Even in Pre-K it was important to me that I did well in school. Doing great in school was never a choice, but it was more so a rule. Failure in school was, and still is, never an option because I literally come from nothing, therefore I have no choice but to work hard in school so that I can eventually become something great. Education has always been a main priority in our household because neither of my grandparents graduated high school. My granddad couldn't even read until he got well into his adult years and my grandparents didn't want this for me or my brother. Therefore, they drilled into us at an early age that no matter what happens we should always put God and education first.

Elementary school was really a breeze, as I was always on Honor Roll without even trying. Academically, elementary school wasn't a challenge at all. I loved award ceremonies because I knew I'd receive several awards. Middle school was different because I was placed in a cluster with other overachievers, so now I had competition. Friendly competition, but nonetheless competition. There weren't as many middle school award ceremonies as there were in elementary school, but I still received awards. I was being academically challenged and honestly, I liked it. Eventually I got used to the challenge until it was no longer a challenge, and middle school soon became like elementary school — a walk in the park that required little to no effort.

High school was seriously different. I'm a junior now and I'm still not fully adjusted to high school. Yes, I'm used to waking up early, I'm used to the people, and I'm used to my schedule, but I'm not used to the workload. This was totally unlike middle and elementary school, where the work was easy. Every year the workload gets harder. Some days I feel like giving up on everything. Dropping out has crossed my mind more than once, and I am not talking about just dropping out of advanced classes and going to General Education classes: I'm talking about dropping out and never returning to school again!

You probably think I'm overexaggerating, but I'm not. Every adult I know says high school is supposed to be the best, most fun years of my life, but these past three years have been the exact opposite. So far, high school has been nothing but stress for me and fun is very rare. While there have been some good moments, high school has not been all sunshine and rainbows. At this point, I'm just ready for it to be May 2020 so I can graduate already.

If you're wondering why I'm *so* stressed and *so* ready to graduate, it is because the main cause of all my stress is the amount of work my school puts on me. See, the thing is, I don't take regular classes; I take the most rigorous classes my school has to offer. I don't think I should give the name of the college-prep program, because I don't want to get in trouble for copyright infringement, but just know they're not Advanced Placement classes; they're much harder than that. Normally, you have to audition to even get into the program that I am in. During the auditions, you have to come to the school and write a paper about whatever topic they decide to give you.

However, I didn't even have to audition to be in the college-prep program. My middle school teacher recommended me, and one day I got a letter in the mail that said they had checked my transcript and I was qualified to be in the program. My grandmother and I signed the papers, and that was all it took. Prior to us signing the papers, we'd only heard good things about the program, and we knew that it was going to be more difficult than the regular General Ed classes, but when I got to high school and started taking the classes, I soon realized it was definitely more than I expected.

Ninth grade year was great. I flourished socially, but I was floundering academically. I was passing all my tests and quizzes, but I never did any homework. I made new friends, but my grades dropped. I was no longer "Mya with the straight A's." I wasn't even "Mya with the straight A's and B's." I cared about my grades, but I didn't put any effort into doing much of the work. For the first time, I was being assigned homework for each class every night, and the homework counted. It wasn't just the basic homework either. For the first time in my life, it actually required effort, and I wanted nothing to do with it!

Whenever we got progress reports, it never really bothered or worried me. I didn't really care because, after all, they weren't reports cards. However, when I finally got my report card, I rethought my whole life! My school only gave out one report card at the end of the school year, so all the way up to that point I was "living my best life." Sad to say, I was having fun, and as a result I wasn't really focused on my grades.

Any of the teachers I had freshman year can attest to how I played entirely too much. For example, during class one of my teachers told me to go into the hallway and to stop playing around, but instead of listening, I laughed. I couldn't contain my laughter, so the teacher made me stay in the hallway for a few minutes. I was eventually allowed back into the class, but I had to move to another seat. Overall, I was an immature, goofy freshman, and the report card I received that May showed it. I walked away from freshman year with a 3.2 GPA. I understand that this would be good for some people, but I was devastated because I knew I could do so much better. I knew I had to get my entire life together or I'd possibly ruin my chances at going to a good college.

Seeing that 3.2 on paper motivated me to go even harder during my sophomore year. The first semester of sophomore year was rough though. I started out with a positive attitude and I was looking forward to the year because I knew I was going to do better than I did freshman year. This is actually how things started out, but then everything took a turn for the worst. The week before Thanksgiving break, I got into a fight. This incident is still shocking to me because the girl and I were pretty nice to each other before everything went down.

One day she just came to school with a stank attitude and I asked her a question. Her response was rude, so I said something about it, even though my friends told me not to. After all, she had no reason to come at me like that! She hit me first, and I don't care what school policy says, if somebody hits me, I'm hitting them back with no hesitation, because that's what my grandparents taught me to do. Unfortunately, after the fight I had to go to a retina specialist, and he told me that I couldn't afford to fight anymore because my eyes are really sensitive. He told me that I could've gone blind at any moment, but he gave me a laser eye treatment to prevent blindness. It was my mother who caused the initial problems with my eyes, but I'll get into that later.

I was suspended for three days after the fight, and I was very mad at myself for even entertaining the girl I fought. After a fight in seventh grade, I promised myself that I'd never let anybody bring me out of my character like that again, but I broke that promise. In both fights the other person hit me first, but I still felt really bad for even letting another person have the ability to bring me out of character. When I came back to school after the fight, I was really bitter towards the girl, but after a few days I decided to let it go. After all, I was going to have to see her every day for the rest of the school year. We kept it cordial with each other, which was absolutely great.

For the rest of the first semester of sophomore year I worked my butt off, and I was a much better student than I was freshman year. I put all my effort into school and almost all of my homework. Yes, I skipped a few assignments, but those weren't enough to severely drop my grades like they did freshman year. At the end of the semester, when it was time to take finals, something else happened. While taking my math final I got in trouble for cheating, which caused me to get a zero on the test. I was left with a C in the class. Thank God I had an A in the class prior to the final, because if I didn't, I would have failed the class completely.

Sophomore year, the school switched to half credits, meaning we received two report cards — one in December and one in May. On my December report card, I had five A's, one B, and one C. After the first semester of sophomore year I did some serious self-reflection and decided that next semester would be better. Sure enough, I improved significantly. I was motivated, and I really put my all into school, because I knew I could be and do so much better than I had previously done. I decided that I wasn't going to let anybody bring me out of my character again, and this time I was adamant about it.

Of course, there was petty drama here and there and sometimes I did feed into it, but nothing escalated into a full-blown argument. When I received my report card in May, for the second semester of sophomore year, I had five A's and two B's. A part of me was glad that there were no C's, and then the other part of me was mad because one of the B's was an 89. That 89 really bothered me and I cried about it because it was *so* close to an A. I beat myself up for a good two weeks because of that 89, but I had to remind myself that I did all that I could possibly do. I did my best and there was no sense in stressing myself out over it because there was nothing I could do to change it anyway. I left sophomore year with a 3.5 GPA, which put me on track to become an Honors graduate.

Sophomore year was really an experience. There were good memories and there were bad memories, but I learned something from both the good and bad. Sophomore year taught me that no matter what happens you can always get up, dust yourself off, and keep going. I always knew that not everyone meant well and that not everyone who smiles in your face is your friend, but sophomore year reiterated that for me. I learned that sometimes the best response is no response at all. Sophomore year also taught me who my real friends were and who would stick around when I needed them most. Real friends push you to become better, and mine did just that.

Chapter 13

The Hardest School Year Ever

Along with learning lessons, during my sophomore year my friends and I created memories that will last a lifetime. I can honestly say that year was the most important year of high school, but it was far from being the most entertaining or the most fun. Although I made some mistakes during my sophomore year, I wouldn't trade it for anything. The lessons I learned from that year will be lessons I'll remember for the rest of my life. Sophomore year pushed me to want to do better for junior year.

I had heard rumors about how junior year was going to be the hardest year we'd ever experience, as it pertains to school, but I never really paid much attention to the rumors because honestly, I didn't think any school year could be worse than the first half of sophomore year. However, I was quickly proven to be wrong because although junior year is only halfway over as I write this book, it's been by far the hardest school year I've experienced to this day! I get stressed just thinking about it. Junior year has been the most work for not only me, but also my peers who are in the program as well. Junior year has dragged us for filth, for real.

Junior year has been an immense amount of work, and I'm convinced this program doesn't want us to have any social lives at all! We're used to having a lot of work, but not *this* much work. This program's classes load us with more work than we would receive in college. Apparently, they're trying to teach us time management skills, and they're also trying to teach us how to cope with stress. Well, honey, I'm not doing a good job at coping with this stress at all! I'm almost always on the verge of a mental breakdown.

My mama is always receiving texts from me about those mental breakdowns, too. The workload is no joke and it will honestly drive you crazy sometimes, but we recover. In addition to having to adjust to the workload, we've had to adjust to this eight-class schedule. The General Ed program has seven classes, but the college-prep program I am in gives us eight. As a result, I have two sixth periods. We alternate days, resulting in half of us going to biology on Mondays and the other half going to the other sixth period, and we switch the next day.

I'm personally used to going to every class, every day, so it took some getting used to. Science is definitely not my strong suit, therefore at times I wish that we went to science every day, because it does get hard when I have to go over the notes at home when half the time I don't even understand what they're saying. Science doesn't come naturally for me, and I really do struggle with that class. We just took finals last week and thankfully, I could exempt my Biology, Spanish, Sculpture, Dance, and Literature finals. As for the finals I had to take, I did excellent on my U.S. History final: I made a 98.

Social Studies is hands down my favorite subject. I could read a history book or watch a good documentary for hours! On my math final, however, I didn't do as well: I failed it with a 59. I had a feeling that I was going to fail because my grade in math had been up and down all semester long. For example, I'd do really good on one test and then fail the next, so I knew I probably wasn't going to do as great on that math final, and my prediction was absolutely correct.

I know it sounds bad, but I didn't really care about failing that math test. As long as I was still passing the class, I didn't care. I was honestly worn out. The semester was just crazy. I've never had so many sleepless nights in my life! This semester really tried me because my stress level has been on ten since a few days after the school year began. I'm elated to finally be on Christmas break because God knows I was just about to give it all up for real. Not only that, but this semester had me questioning my intelligence. I seriously thought I was losing my "smartness." First semester was definitely trying, and I absolutely thought about quitting on more than one occasion, but I didn't. I've been in this college-prep program way too long to quit now. The only way I'll leave this program is if I'm forced to due to flunking out, which I won't allow to happen.

Next semester I'm coming back even harder though. I'm using this break to get some much-needed rest, because I know when we go back to school, there will be no such thing as rest. I plan to put my best foot forward in everything I do from this point forward, because I have the ability to be great — I just have to tap into it. I'm believing that although next semester will be trying, it will be rewarding as well. In the end, I think my grades will show that all my hard work paid off. I'm proud of myself for making it to this point despite all the odds that were against me. My mother didn't graduate from high school, but I will. I'm believing that I'll graduate with honors as well, which will make my grandparents so proud! As long as I keep my grades up and stay disciplined, I will graduate with honors.

Senior year will no doubt be memorable, but it'll be a lot of hard work as well. I'll get through it as I always have. I've overcome a lot of things in my life and high school will soon be one of the things I can add to that list. I know firsthand how it can be really hard to focus in school, especially when you have situations going on at home, but it's possible. It takes a lot of strength to ignore what's going on in your personal life and place all your focus on school, but I know the end result will be so worth it.

There have been times when I would come to school and be totally zoned out in first period, and by the time the class was over I would realize I didn't hear a thing my teacher said. I realized that this wasn't good at all, therefore I had to find ways that I could get my focus on track. One thing that helps me is listening to gospel on the way to school and while I'm waiting for the bell to ring. Music is my thing, and I'm glad I found something that works in helping me to remain focused. I read sometimes as well because reading is another good way for me to calm down. I think all teenagers should remind themselves from time to time that school isn't social hour, but we're there to get an education.

Also, I think it is important to remember to be kind to others, because there were times when I'd come to school and internally I was a mess, but I didn't show it. Unfortunately, people would sometimes say some mean stuff to me, but I'm a strong person and I can take insults every now and then. However, one time somebody said something about me and I started crying. It wasn't the insult that really bothered me; it was more so the fact that I was thinking about something else that was really bothering me and that triggered me. That was really a rare moment because I hardly ever break down like that in front of people, but that just goes to show that even the strongest people have a breaking point.

Adults sometimes fail to realize that school is different from when they may have been in high school, especially for those of us who take advanced classes. I just wish adults would stop assuming that school is easy! I want to scream at adults sometimes and tell them to stop assuming that we're stressing out over nothing, because we're not! I want to tell adults that if we (teenagers) come to you and tell you that school is stressing us out, please don't yell, because sometimes we are on the verge of a mental breakdown. We deal with a lot as teenagers. We're human and we stress sometimes too, so stop minimizing our feelings and emotions! Sometimes, instead of the fussing we need a hug or a "how was school?" We need as much encouragement as possible because sometimes we don't have any motivation at all.

We often have to keep ourselves motivated, which is a very hard task. Hearing "I'm proud of you" or "you're doing great, keep going" goes a long way. I understand that as parents sometimes you all have to fuss at us, but sometimes we need you to be understanding because school can be a greater burden than many adults realize.

Chapter 14

The Best Thanksgiving Ever

If someone were to ask me what my favorite holiday is, I'd probably say Christmas. However, if someone asked me which holiday is most *important* to me, I'd no doubt say Thanksgiving. I understand that the good Christian answer would be to say that Christmas is the most important holiday because we celebrate Jesus' birth, but I said what I said: Thanksgiving is the most important holiday *to me,* Mya Joyce. Thanksgiving is a time when families come together, feast, and just enjoy each other's company. Well, most families anyway. My family is one of the families that doesn't necessarily function like a normal family, but we'll get more into that later in this chapter. Thanksgiving for me is not just about the food and the fellowship, there's more to it than just that for a very special reason.

You may or may not remember from earlier chapters, but Thanksgiving Day 2005 was the day I came home after being away from my grandparents for nearly a year. That year was the worst year of my life, and I've dealt with some things since then, but nothing comes close to how bad that experience was for me. When I was finally allowed to come back home, I was ecstatic! That day, even though it was thirteen years ago, will always be a day that I will forever remember and be grateful for. It was no doubt the happiest day of my life, and it was most definitely one of the most important days of my life. Who knows where I'd be or what I'd be doing if I had never been able to come back home.

The first Thanksgiving I can remember celebrating is the Thanksgiving when I came home. I was only three years old at the time, but I still remember that day like it was yesterday. It was very cold, in a Georgia-cold kind of way, because we don't like cold weather in the south. The leaves were just starting to fall off the trees. I remember the leaves because I was fascinated with how many there were on the ground. When the social worker, Ms. A, arrived at my grandparents' house with me, I couldn't contain my excitement! I got out of the car as quickly as I could and ran to the door. Not the front door, but the back door. I also remember informing Ms. A of how we didn't use the front door, but we used the back door instead. I really don't know why we used the back door instead of the front door, but we still do it today even though we no longer live in the same house.

My grandparents had no idea that I was coming home, and they were just as surprised as I was when I got there. When I knocked on the door, my grandmother's face turned from completely sad to overjoyed in a matter of seconds. She started screaming and even shed a few tears. My grandfather came to see what she was screaming about and then they both started screaming together. My grandfather was so happy to see me! In fact, he almost shed some tears too. They really weren't expecting me to come home at all, especially not before Thanksgiving. They were at their wits' end, and I saw it all over my grandmother's face when she opened that door.

My grandparents still had faith in God, but you could tell that they were really worn out. After we'd hugged and kissed and calmed down, we realized Ms. A was still there and she had seen all of this. She had a shocked look on her face, which was probably because she basically witnessed life come back to me. She was used to me being a sad, depressed child, so when she saw me light up and actually display happiness it was all new to her.

Ms. A had to speak with my grandparents before she could leave, and I really didn't pay much attention to anything she said. I was just happy to be back home, and I didn't care what she had to say! I do remember her saying that child services would send someone to the house every once in a while to do checkups to make sure that I was being properly taken care of. After Ms. A left, my grandparents and I enjoyed each other's presence. My grandmother started cooking. She explained that prior to my arrival she didn't plan on cooking anything because there was no reason to. Before I came home that day, my grandparents were by themselves, and although it was Thanksgiving, no family had come over. All seven of their children were either out of town or they just had something better to do, I suppose. I knew where my mother was though. She was running around town with her boyfriend, but that was the usual.

It was just the three of us and we were OK with that. We were completely OK with the fact that our family didn't care to come over, and I was fine with the fact that my mother didn't show up either. However, I still cannot for the life of me understand why she would choose her boyfriend, Tyrone, over her own parents! I probably won't ever understand it, but I know on that Thanksgiving it was the last thing on my mind. It was almost like the past didn't matter for a moment, but we were simply basking in the happiness we received from being reunited with each other for good. It was exactly what the three of us needed. This was the first Thanksgiving I remember, and it is the best one I've experienced to this day.

My most recent Thanksgiving was definitely one to remember, but it left me with some good memories and some bad ones as well. The good part is that my mama and her husband came to visit me. My grandfather's best friend's son is my mama's husband, and he came to spend time with my granddad. They came all the way from New York just to see us! I honestly didn't think they would actually come because I hadn't known Mrs. Holmes for that long, and though I trusted her I also knew that she could probably change her mind. Another reason I didn't think they would come was because nobody has ever done such a thing for me. When we picked them up from the airport on Wednesday and brought them to Macon, we took them out to eat and we just bonded with each other. I really enjoyed myself.

Normally, I don't like people, but with Mrs. Holmes it was different. It was like I'd been knowing her all my life, which is probably because I've told her my whole life story and we talk every day. The entire time she was here, I never left her side. The only time I did leave her side was when we were eating because I had to eat at another other table, which made me mad. However, I kept it "cute" because we had company. Not only did I finally get to see my mama in person, but it was such an amazing thing to see my granddad and her husband talking. They really do encourage each other; their friendship is so amazing! One day I hope to have a friendship like theirs because I really admire what they have.

Bonding with my mama was the good part of the trip. I was honestly just happy to be in her presence; she's like my best friend. I hadn't been that happy in a while, but as usual something interfered with my happiness. To a certain extent it worked, but my mama wasn't having it, so she cheered me up. As usual, my biological mother was getting on my nerves, but she wasn't the one who triggered me on this Thanksgiving. I won't say who, but a certain family member sent me a series of mean texts, and he had me questioning my sanity. I was really trying to figure out what I did to make him hate me so much! Like dang, you're family so you're supposed to actually love me, not send me hateful text messages — especially not on Thanksgiving!

He's one of the family members that more than likely doesn't know why Thanksgiving is so important to me. After receiving those texts, I became really sad. In spite of all the good things going on around me, I could feel depression coming over me. It really bothered me to the point where I didn't even eat as much as I usually do. As usual, nobody noticed that I was feeling this way. However, when my mama and her husband were about to leave our house to go back to their hotel, we started talking.

"Are you OK?" she asked.

I guess I was looking sad or acting as if something was wrong. I just broke down for real and cried. I told her what was wrong, and she gave me a hug — and that hug was everything! She reassured me that none of the things that have happened and were happening to me were my fault. She listened to me and comforted me, which was exactly what I needed. Sadly, I normally keep everything to myself, which usually drives me crazy, and the outcome of that is horrible.

"I don't know what *that* was because thugs don't cry," I said with a laugh.

We both started laughing, and to this day I've been repeating that to myself when I feel sad. When we were done having our moment, she said that she wanted to take me to the mall because she knew how important Thanksgiving was for me. She ultimately wanted me to end the day on a positive note, which made me so happy and it really made me feel loved. We went to the mall, spent some quality time together, and I spent all her money! I'm kidding, but that definitely cheered me up and took my mind off what had happened earlier in the day.

I even got to ask her some questions that had really been on my mind. The best thing wasn't about the fact that she spent money on me, but it was more so that although she was tired (she even had to stop and buy a Red Bull energy drink), she wanted to spend time with me. She could have gone back to the hotel with her husband and went to sleep, but she chose to spend time with me, and for that I will be forever grateful.

This most recent Thanksgiving started out as the worst Thanksgiving I'd ever had, but it soon became one of my favorites. Just like my first Thanksgiving, I will forever remember this one too. My mama really flew all the way from New York just to come see little 'ole me. To some it may not seem like anything special because people take flights all the time. True, people take flights all the time, but nobody had ever taken a flight just to spend time with me! Therefore, to me it was a really special Thanksgiving. I'm the type of person who gets happy about the little things. It takes much more than money to excite me or make me feel like you care. I met my mama in person this Thanksgiving, and she helped change it from the worst to the best.

Chapter 15

Mama Issues

In the beginning of the book, I said my biological mother was the cause of me being depressed and having low self-esteem. You know how people say, "nobody will have your back like your mama" or "nobody will love you like your mama?" Well, for me and my life, those type of sayings couldn't be further from the truth. My mother has never had my back, and to this day I sometimes still view her as an enemy. We don't have any type of relationship, much less a mother-daughter relationship. I don't even want a relationship with her, to be honest.

I know that she's the person who gave birth to me, therefore I'm supposed to respect her, but she doesn't deserve my respect! Maybe one day my heart will change towards her, but for now I just can't find it in my heart to forgive her for all the terrible things she's said and done to me. To be honest, when I was younger, even before I was taken into child protective services, I never liked my mother. Prior to me going to child services, I spent most of my time with my grandparents. My grandparents took care of me while she was in the streets with her boyfriend getting high on drugs and who knows what else. When I did go to my mother's house, her boyfriend was always with her and she probably could care less about me being there.

My mother's boyfriend was her main and only focus. I think she only came to get me from time to time because my grandparents wanted her to take care of her own child. They wanted to spend time with me, but at the same time they wanted my mother to take care of her responsibilities as a mother. I believe they wanted her to feel what it was like to be a mother in the hopes that she wouldn't want to have another baby, seeing that she was still young.

As a result of her being away so often, I always sensed that my mother never cared about me. Although I was a young child, I felt like a burden when I was around her and her boyfriend. The times I did spend the night at my mother's house, I slept on the floor most of the time. My grandparents even purchased a bed for me to sleep in at her house, but my mother and her boyfriend always ended up sleeping in it when he was at home at night. As a result, they would sleep in the bed while I slept on the floor like a dog.

I was one of those kids who could pick up on vibes, and if I felt like you didn't like me, I didn't want to be around you. Therefore, I soon had no desire to be around my mother. There's a picture I have of my mother, my grandma and me, which was taken before I even got taken away by child services. In the photo, you can see all over my face that I did not want to be in a picture with my mother! I was sitting as close to my grandma as I possibly could be. My body language in the photo is proof that this hatred and bitterness toward my mother is nothing new. I've felt like this for a long time, but I'm just now getting the courage to speak about it.

My mother was causing problems in my life before I was even born. For example, I have terrible eyesight to the point where I'm almost blind without my glasses. One of my eyes is worse than the other, but both are really bad. The cause? My mother. The eye doctor told me that my mother drank alcohol or did stuff she had no business doing while she was pregnant with me. I could've probably had good eyesight had it not been for her foolishness, but that's the earliest reason I can think of as to why I hate her so much.

When I first went to child services, I thought that my mother would finally pay attention to me for once. I thought that since it was an argument between her and her boyfriend Tyrone that got me taken away, she would at least fight for me to come back home to her. Unfortunately, that wasn't the case at all. She didn't come for me, and I think that's what broke my heart the most. My own mother didn't fight for me! However, she fought several females over that no-good boyfriend of hers. She forgave Tyrone for things he had done to her, but she eventually lost him. Tyrone was found dead after being shot multiple times in a shoot-out.

Before his death, Tyrone was the person she chose to chase instead of chasing her three-year-old daughter. Man, that's foul, and I don't care how many excuses people try to make for her — IT WAS FOUL! It broke my heart. She chose a man, that wasn't even my father, over me, and I'll never be OK with that! I get it, we all make poor decisions when we're young, but I don't see every teen mother abandoning their child. I feel like once she felt grown enough to lie down with somebody and risk having a child, she should've been grown enough to take care of and love on that child she created.

Yes, I understand that my mother was young, but what kind of excuse is that? Some people feel like she was just young and dumb, but why did it continue after she grew up?

She continued to disrespect me even throughout her adult years. Truthfully, my mother was my first bully. The woman who was supposed to protect me and love me more than anybody. The person who was supposed to have my back more than anybody else was the same one I needed to be protected from. Sadly, I never got that protection, which is why I suppose I still can't get over this to this day. While she never physically abused me, she definitely verbally abused me, so when I say I needed to be protected, I'm talking about from verbal abuse, not physical.

The first time she called me fat, my feelings were hurt. I've always been very insecure about my weight and hearing it from the person who gave birth to me really hurt me. After calling me fat, she didn't stop there. She continued calling me names, and it's almost like she got pleasure from doing it. To this day, she still calls me names and it's painful for me. She also calls me stupid and that particular insult really agitates me. You can call me any name in the book and it wouldn't really bother me, but if you want to really get a reaction out of me, call me stupid and watch me go off!

Imagine repeatedly getting called names by your own mother. Eventually the constant disrespect got to me and I decided that I was going to treat her the same way she treats me. She made me miserable, so I was going to make her feel it as well. Since the day I made that decision to make her feel my pain, I've continued to treat her that way. Why should I show her any respect at this point? I know the Bible says to "honor thy father and thy mother" but I feel like you have to earn the title of "father" or "mother." In my opinion, you can't just make a baby and be called a father, and you can't just birth a baby and be called a mother. She hasn't earned the title as my mother; therefore, I feel like she deserves every bit of hatred and disrespect that I give her.

She calls me stupid, so I'm determined to show her what stupid really is! What I do to her is nothing compared to what she's done to her parents though. For instance, one time she pulled a knife on my grandfather. Yes, a real knife! In fact, she acted like she was really going to kill him! She used to show up to our old apartment and beat on our door like she was crazy. She didn't even care that her two children were there because she was probably too high off drugs to even realize what she was doing.

My mother would come by the house and yell loudly at my grandparents for no reason. Every time she did this, my grandparents would get their anointing oil and they always threw some of it on her and started pleading the blood of Jesus. She would always leave when they started doing that. She started coming so often to the point where she eventually got banned because my grandparents wouldn't let her spend the night with us. As a result, she would sleep on the stairs in the apartment building because she had nowhere else to go. I remember being embarrassed because my brother and I would go outside to the play area with the other kids and they'd say, "we saw y'all mama sleeping on the stairs again." This was embarrassing, to say the least, and I did not want to be associated with that woman at all.

One time my mother got arrested for sleeping in the stairwells. Honestly, I think my grandparents were kind of relieved. Not because she had gotten locked up, but because they knew she wouldn't be wandering the streets for days or weeks. This happened on more than one occasion, and each time it happened I remember feeling completely embarrassed. Each time she got arrested, the entire neighborhood would talk about it. I was around nine years old at the time, but it was very traumatic for me. Picture being nine years old, and your mother is beating on the door like she's crazy, screaming loudly, and threatening your grandparents. It's not a pretty picture, is it?

Then there was the time she thought it was OK to hit my grandmother in front of me and my cousins. By this time, we had moved into a house and I was eleven or twelve years old. One night my mother came in high on drugs and she was just being her normal crazy self. My grandmother went downstairs to see what she was doing because my mother was being very loud. My grandmother told her to turn her music down and to stop being loud, but my mother decided to become confrontational with my grandmother! I heard her all the way upstairs yelling and repeatedly telling my grandma that she was grown. She was definitely grown age-wise, but mentally she was no older than me.

She kept yelling at my grandma, and I decided to go downstairs to see what all the fuss was about. By the time I got down the stairs, my two cousins, who were living with us at the time, had already left their rooms to see what was going on. My cousins and I are very protective of my grandma, so I was standing there watching to make sure my mother didn't decide to get too bold. My grandfather was asleep during the altercation, and nobody thought to wake him up, because we didn't think it would get as far as it eventually did. There they were, arguing with each other for a few minutes because my grandmother wasn't about to let my mother think she could do whatever she wanted in her house. I guess my mother got so angry to the point where she pushed my grandmother, and I don't know why she thought that was OK. That was a big mistake because as soon as she did that, my cousin went to town on her!

Chapter 16

She Deserved That Punch

My mother tried to fight back, but my cousin beat her up GOOD! I bet you she won't ever lay a finger on my grandmother again after that whooping she received! When my cousin started beating her up, I ran upstairs and told my grandfather that my mother had hit my grandmother, and he was extremely upset. He went downstairs to handle business, but by the time he got there my cousin had already done what needed to be done. After my cousin finished beating up my mother, my grandparents did their original routine of pleading the blood and throwing oil and once again, she ran off.

Recently, my grandmother went on an overnight trip with some family members. My mother, who was now living with us, came home around 7:00 p.m. We heard the door slam loudly downstairs. At first, we thought nothing of it because my mother had a habit of slamming the door every once in a while. However, the thing that aggravated us was the fact that she kept opening and slamming the door. In a matter of five minutes, she had opened and closed the door like twenty times. This was all happening around the time my grandfather gets ready to go to bed, so her slamming the door repeatedly really bothered him. At our house there's a door and then the steps, but as soon as he opened the door to go down the steps, we immediately smelled the strong scent of weed.

Anybody who knows my grandparents will tell you that they don't tolerate the smoking of anything in their house — no cigarettes, no weed, no nothing! When he smelled weed downstairs, he was already kind of pissed off because when she started living with us, they made it perfectly clear that no smoking of any kind was allowed in our house. My brother and I followed my granddad downstairs, and even though he doesn't need us to protect him, we wanted to be there just in case she did anything stupid like she normally does.

"Are you smoking in my house?" my grandfather calmly and politely asked.

"No, I ain't smoking," she replied, looking him dead in his face.

I was shocked! Who lies to somebody's face like that when we all clearly know that you've been smoking? My grandfather was completely chill until she started speaking again.

"And if I was?" she said defiantly.

It was at that moment that I knew things were about to escalate because my grandfather cannot tolerate people talking to him any kind of way. After that response from her, he nicely told her to step outside because he didn't allow that in his house. My mother didn't move. My granddad decided to politely take her outside because it was clear she had been smoking downstairs, and he was not about to let her do that in his house. When he got her outside, she decided to act a fool, yelling all kinds of crazy things. Then she did the unthinkable: she hit my grandfather!

I knew my mother had to be high out of her mind because what possessed her to even lay a finger on my granddad when he could easily hurt her? When she hit him, my grandfather restrained her by putting her on the ground. Despite him having her under control, she was trying to hit him back the entire time. I stood there in shock, wondering to myself how my mother could be this crazy! After he finally let her go, she got up and once again ran off. My grandfather yelled for us to call the police, which I had already done because I was scared that he might kill her.

My granddad is really big on respect in his house, so if you decide to hit him, especially in his home, you're making a big mistake. When the police came, my mother made a scene and made it seem like my grandfather just beat her up. She even said that my grandfather wasn't her dad, and that's when the police knew something was wrong with her because they said she looks just like him. After saying he wasn't her father, she made this big deal about getting her clothes and other belongings from downstairs. My grandfather let her get all her things and the police took her to a mental health place nearby.

Unfortunately, she checked herself out the next day and of all places, she decided to come back to our house! It's been several times when she acted like she was leaving, but she always came back, and I'll never understand why my grandparents allowed it. I hope one day I can find it in my heart to forgive her like they have because they've literally been through hell and back with that woman and they still love her.

Those are just a few examples of how poorly my mother has treated her parents. The little petty stuff I sometimes do to her is nowhere near equal to how disrespectful she is to her parents. Even if it was equal to what she's done, the difference between her and my grandparents is that she deserves it, and they don't. I can only think of one situation where I did something to her that was serious. One day she kept bothering me by calling me ugly and fat, and then laughing about it all throughout the day. I was honestly angry and just fed up with her! I didn't want her in my face at all!

One of my pet peeves is certain people touching me. If I know you don't like me, then why on God's green earth are you touching me? In this particular instance, I told my mother not to touch me and she decided to do it anyway. I have the type of personality where if I tell you not to do something to me, I expect you not to do it because I can really turn into a whole other person. When she touched me that day, I punched her as hard as I possibly could! I could tell it hurt by the way she looked at me, but I didn't care.

Of course, my grandparents told me that I shouldn't hit her, because regardless of what she does or says, she's still my mother. I disagree with that. Like I said before, I believe the title of mother has to be earned and she has done everything but be a mother. I wouldn't even say she's been a bad mother because she hasn't been a mother, ever. In my opinion, she deserves every bad attitude I give her. She deserved that punch. All the disrespect I give her is something she absolutely deserves. I suppose disrespecting her is my way of expressing my anger towards her. I'm so angry and I want her to feel every bit of bitterness she's caused.

My mother will never know all the tears I cried and still cry. She will never realize all the nights I stayed up when everybody else thought I was asleep, but I was really up trying to figure out why my mother didn't love me. All the meals I skipped, that nobody ever noticed, because I believed and still do believe that I'm fat. All these years of depression and low self-esteem because the person who was supposed to love me the most was the one causing me the most pain. All these years of being scared to even look people in their eyes when talking to them. All these years of being scared to even let somebody in because I'm afraid they'll just turn around and hurt me like she did. All these years of feeling like everything was my fault because of the way she treated me!

People don't see my innermost feelings; they just see me being mean to her and assume I'm just being disrespectful for no reason. There's absolutely a reason behind me treating her the way I do, and that's part of the reason why I decided to write this book. I wanted to tell *my* story so people can stop assuming they know everything about me, because they don't. People assume my mother is sweet and quiet, but that couldn't be further from the truth. I don't know my mother as "mama" or "mom" — that's why I call her by her first name.

My grandparents don't even have a problem with me calling my mother by her first name, so why do other people care? I refuse to give somebody who has been tormenting me my whole life the title of mother or mama. I refuse because that to me feels like I would be condoning her behavior and not holding her accountable for her wrongs. I probably will never call my mother "mama" and that's just my truth right now. Everything she has done to me still replays in my head every night, and I'm just thankful that I haven't lost my mind.

As I'm getting older, I'm realizing that it's important for me to let this hate go as soon as possible, which is why I wrote this book. I wrote this book to help me heal. I don't want to be well into my thirties and still harboring hatred in my heart from something that happened years ago. I don't like being this angry, bitter person, and I don't like being depressed either. I realize that eventually I'll have to forgive my mother, but as of now I haven't.

Chapter 17

Is Depression A Choice?

There have been times and still are times when I question my sanity. Sometimes I really do think I'm crazy because of my thoughts and how much I break down. During the day, I'm normally able to keep my composure and not show any sign of emotion, but at night it's like I'm a different person. It's as if everything comes back to haunt me at night. I think about everything over and over again, until I find myself crying. Most of the time they aren't tears of sadness, but they are more so tears of anger. I get very angry at not only my mother, but I also get upset with myself for caring more than I think I should.

A year ago, I would never cry as much as I do now, but I'm becoming an overly emotional being and I don't like it at all. Crying makes me feel extremely weak, and I know that's not true, but I still don't like crying. People think I'm this strong individual and truly I'm not. I don't think I'm strong at all because I can barely go a night without crying myself to sleep. I can't even go a day without feeling angry every time

I look at my mother! I just don't get how she can live with herself after everything she's done.

Maybe she forgot, but I sure haven't. In fact, I won't ever forget. Have you ever cried to the point where you could hardly catch your breath? I have. It happens to me almost every night because of my mother. It's almost like I can't escape the thoughts. As I've said before, the thoughts haunt me, which is why I sometimes think I'm crazy. For the longest time I wanted to die because my mother didn't love me. I didn't want to live because I was sick and tired of crying every night. I was tired of being angry, and I was just tired of life all together.

It got to the point where I started to cut myself. I was careful to do it in places where I knew no one would see or notice. It took me a lot of courage to even write this because for the longest time I didn't want anybody to know. I was afraid of what my friends and other people would think of me if they knew what I was really feeling on the inside. I'm finally ready to tell everyone what was going on because I think I can help someone else to speak up about their private emotional struggles.

I'm happy to say that I no longer cut myself. In fact, I haven't done it in months. I think I was able to stop because I found another outlet — writing. I no longer want to die either, but sometimes I still do wish I could stop existing for a moment, if that makes sense. When I started writing this book, I was afraid of being transparent. I figured that I'd only tell some stuff and keep some stuff private. I really went back and forth with myself because I was genuinely afraid of what people would think of me. Would my friends think I was fake because I've never told them my story? Would fellow church members look at me differently because I questioned God? Would my family dislike me even more than they already do? All of these questions entered my head when I first started writing, I originally decided that I would only tell the bare minimum.

I'm relieved that I changed my mind. I am tired of faking like I am OK when I am internally dying. One thing that really encouraged me to change my mind and tell my full story was hearing people around me say things like: "depression isn't real" or "depression is a choice because you can really just snap out of it." When I hear things like this it makes me angry because how can someone say that? Depression *is* real, and I feel like unless you've experienced it, you'll never truly know what it's like. I also believe that whether they like to admit it or not, almost everybody has experienced some form of depression at some point in their life.

When people say things like "depression is a choice," I believe it discourages many teenagers from speaking out, myself included. People tend to judge not only depressed teenagers, but also depressed people in general because they feel like depression is something you can just shake off. This is also one of the reasons why I was afraid to be totally transparent — I was afraid I would be judged. After a while I realized that the need for other teenagers' voices to be heard, as well as mine, was bigger and more important than any fear I could have.

Self-harm is hardly ever spoken of where I come from, so when I started cutting myself, I thought I was crazy. I thought I was losing my mind but really, I was only expressing what I felt inside. Self-harm is simply a harmful way of expressing the negative emotion that one feels inside. Teenagers are typically the ones that self-harm because usually no one cares to talk to us about what we are going through, and we hold our feelings and emotions inside until they drive us crazy.

I've had several people come into my life and they probably cared, but at some point in time they ended up giving up on me. After being given up on several times, I decided that I'd simply stick to keeping everything to myself because what's the point in even attempting to vent to someone if they're just going to give up on me in a couple of days or weeks. All of this changed when I met my mama. I've literally told her everything and she still hasn't given up on me. I know what it is like to feel alone and have no one to talk to, because that was my life for a long time. Thankfully, now I have my mama.

To anyone feeling depressed that is reading this, please reach out to someone. Make sure you can trust that person first, and whenever you feel comfortable you can start telling them more and more. Trust me, I know what it feels like to not trust anyone because you feel like everyone is out to get you, or you feel like no one will really care. However, I can honestly say deciding to confide in my mama was one of the best decisions I've ever made in my life!

I'm tired of faking like my life is something that it's not. Most of my friends think that my parents are married and that I live happily with my mother, father, and brother. That is far from the truth, and I'm kind of disappointed in myself for letting them believe that for as long as they have. Some of my friends have even spent the night at my house before and they assumed that I was just with my grandparents for the weekend. When they saw my mother and asked who she was, without thinking I would tell them she was aunt. They never asked about her again. I know that probably makes me a bad person, but I didn't want anybody to know who my mother was. The only people at school who know I live with my grandparents are my teachers and a few people who went to elementary school with me.

The counselor at my school may know why I live with my grandparents, but honestly, I'm not sure if she does. All

I know is that one day she pulled me out of class and said somebody told her I wanted to kill myself. For three days in a row she pulled me out of class. This felt completely pointless because her counseling methods were ineffective, in my opinion. Maybe it's just me but telling me that I have such good grades isn't really going to help me stop having suicidal thoughts. She even made me sign a contract that said I wouldn't kill myself, which I thought was completely unnecessary because if I did end up killing myself, then what?

Were they going to put my dead body in jail because I breached a contract that said I wouldn't kill myself? That situation was just so funny to me and it's crazy because I still don't know who told her that I said I wanted to kill myself. It was odd because although my self-esteem was low, I wasn't having suicidal thoughts at that time. In fact, I wouldn't have dared to tell anybody about suicidal thoughts — even if I did have them.

While writing this book, I went through and still am going through an array of emotions. Writing inspired me to be more open and honest with a few of my friends. I told them some of my story and one of my friends can strongly relate to me. For example, we both have toxic mothers. Never in a million years would I have thought that I'd be telling anyone my story, and I would've never thought that one of my friends could relate to me. We still talk and check on each other to make sure we're OK. Telling some of my friends about my situation made me feel better and my friends even started confiding in me about what was going on in their lives. Even though our situations are different, there are similarities in each of our stories.

None of my classmates or friends ever really knew what was going on in my life because I've always been good at hiding my emotions. I'm usually the one that's always laughing, smiling, and cheering everyone else up. I didn't want anybody to feel sorry for me; I was more so focused on making sure everybody else around me was good. I felt it was my responsibility to remain strong throughout the day no matter what I was feeling, because nobody needed to know my business. I think now that I've shared with a few of my friends how I've been feeling, it gave them the opportunity to share their stories. It goes both ways. I gained comfort from knowing that I wasn't the only one going through something and they did the same. I'm honestly glad I opened up to them, but there's still a lot that they don't know.

There are still some friends that I talk to and see on a daily basis that don't know anything about my personal life. Yeah, they know me, but they don't *know* me. In fact, one of my closest friends doesn't even know about the things I'm writing in this book, and she's one of the friends who has spent the night at my house before. I'm almost always with her, and when we're together it's nothing but fun. However, we've never really sat down and talked about anything meaningful. We usually only share laughs and talk about stuff that isn't really important when we're together. I think she'll be the most surprised when she reads this book because I've never shown any signs of not being "normal." I'm kind of afraid that she'll be mad at me because I didn't tell her sooner. I would understand if she was upset, but hopefully she will be happy that I channeled all my negative feelings into something positive.

I pray that when, or if, they decide to read this book, my friends aren't mad or angry with me but understanding instead. It took a lot for me to even start writing, and it is by far the scariest and hardest thing I've ever had to do! I hope they're just happy I'm finding a way to get past everything that's happened to me. After all, this book wasn't just written for me to find my healing, but to help other teenagers, like my friends, find theirs as well. Like I said in the first chapter, I refuse to become an angry, mentally unstable individual, and this book is one way of preventing that.

Chapter 18

An Old Soul

All these years people have called me "wise" and I've never felt like it. People always tell me that I act and think differently than the average teenager, and I seriously don't think so. I believe the wisdom I have stems from being around my grandparents for so long and from being in church as well. I suppose I've always had an old soul, now that I think about it. I really do love church and believe some of this "wisdom" comes from that environment, but church folk can be some of the most judgmental people. I'm not referring to my church family, but church folk in general. Church folk sometimes are overly religious, in my opinion. I think they sometimes forget that healing is a process.

While I believe in the power of prayer, I don't believe that healing takes place overnight. Church folk preach that suicide is a sin (which kept me from doing it) and that depression is "of the devil." Honestly, church folk can sometimes make people who have suicidal thoughts and struggle with depression feel bad. I feel like if I come to you and tell you

I'm depressed, you can pray for me, but don't tell me that the devil is in me because of how I feel. I don't need to hear that! I need to hear positive things such as how I can overcome depression and how I can suppress these suicidal thoughts.

Preaching to someone is fine and all, but sometimes people just need a hug and a good conversation. By conversation I mean talking and not just saying "have faith" because having faith is hard! Having faith is especially hard when you feel like you have no reason to live, and I know that from personal experience. We sometimes tell people to just believe that things will get better, and we expect that alone to just make everything OK, but it doesn't. I know it sounds crazy but telling somebody to believe doesn't make them believe.

Sometimes we should step down off our religious soap box and have heart-to-heart conversations with people. The church is supposed to be an uplifting place and it's supposed to help broken people, but that can only happen if we change the way that we do things. I'm not saying don't tell people what the Bible says or what God says, because that's exactly what believers should be doing. However, I think we should realize that not everything is a religious matter. Everybody doesn't understand the spiritual realm, especially teenagers.

Don't get me wrong; there are many positive things about going to church. Church is what kept me from killing myself. Sometimes Christians can lack understanding and it comes off as being rude or mean. Those types of Christians give believers as a whole a bad reputation. How can you preach about how much you love God, but you don't even show love to other people? If I wasn't raised in church and I didn't know God for myself, I probably wouldn't even want to be a Christian. Too many Christians claim they love and serve God, but they're the meanest people ever. Who would want to believe in a God who has servants or followers that are mean?

I know this will probably get under some church folk's skin, but to be honest the sinners and worldly folk that are preached against treat young people better than the church folk do! If you felt attacked by that, then maybe you should examine yourself because you just may be one of the church folks I am talking about. Nobody likes a "Christian" with a bad attitude. Let me clarify that I'm not talking about *my* church family specifically, but I'm referring to church in general. I've heard stories from my friends about how they've had bad experiences with church people, which has caused them to never want to go to a church again.

I completely get where my friends are coming from because I've had my own negative experiences. Generally speaking, I think Christians simply have to do better. We have to be a little bit more loving, empathetic, patient, and caring. Trust me, a little love goes a LONG way. Showing love does more good than being judgmental — I promise it does! I've had experiences with both a loving Christian and a judgmental one. They have both impacted my life, but I can honestly say the love helped me. The judgement? Not so much.

This is probably one of the reasons I love being alone. I'm probably one of the only people I know that prefers to be alone, rather than with a crowd of people. Being alone brings me peace, but I must admit that sometimes I get lonely. I like being alone, but I don't like being lonely, if that makes sense. I suppose that's why I was as depressed as I was. I felt like no one loved and cared about me. I know that wasn't true, because I know my grandparents loved me, but those were the only two people who I believed genuinely loved me. My grandparents are very strict, old school, and very religious, therefore I never felt comfortable talking to them about how I was feeling.

For instance, I wouldn't have ever mentioned to either of my grandparents that I wanted to die. I would've gotten lectured about how suicide is a sin and how it's like murder, and I *know* they would've cast those "demons" out of me. I don't blame my grandparents, because that's how they were raised and that's all they know. I was basically left to deal with these feelings alone because I had nobody to talk to about how I was feeling. Like I said before, I honestly thought I was crazy. It was during those times that I wished the most that I had a mother. Seeing that my mother was younger, I should have been able to talk to her about what I was feeling. To be honest, if my mother had been there in the first place, then I wouldn't even be having these feelings.

I legit used to hate myself and I still sometimes do. I hated the way I look, the way I act, and everything about me. My anxiety was horrible, and I used to be scared to even talk to people. I used to have to build up courage to even speak to somebody. Adults would get mad at me because I didn't talk. They thought I was being rude, but I really wasn't. It was like I had to go through an internal battle with myself before I even got the courage to speak out loud. Sometimes I would decide against talking, and I guess that's what made people mad. Have you ever been in class and you knew the answer to a question the teacher asked, but you were too scared to answer — not because you were afraid of being wrong, but because you were just scared to talk?

Yeah, that was me. My feelings would be hurt when people would call me rude when I would walk into a room and not speak. It probably *was* rude, but I was just really afraid back then. Now, I talk much more — especially if I know you and I'm comfortable around you. I still sometimes hate talking in front of people, like when I'm asked to do something at church. I always say "yes," but I still get really nervous sometimes. I think that's natural though, and the more I do talk in front of people, the less nerve-wracking it becomes.

I told myself many negative things back then. For instance, I convinced myself that I wasn't valuable, and that nobody will ever truly love me because my mother doesn't. I also told myself that I won't ever be anything in life. I never thought I was important or valuable, because if I was, then why did my mother leave me? When I hear the saying "nobody will love you like your mother" it hurts me because this doesn't apply to me. For a long time, I thought I wasn't worthy of love because I wasn't pretty enough or skinny enough and because of who my mother is. One of my greatest fears is that I will end up like my mother. I thought I would be a teen mom like her, that I would end up on drugs like her, and that I would fail at life — just like her.

People would always tell me that I look just like my mother, which is understandable because I am her child. They would also always tell me that I act just like she used to act when she was my age, and that right there angers me because when she was my age, she was living a crazy life! As a result, I am actively working to unlearn these negative things that I've taught myself over the years, but it has been far from easy.

Chapter 19

The Black Sheep

For a while I struggled with self-love, and that struggle continues to this day. I thought nobody loved me so why would I love myself? As previously mentioned, I wanted to die because I believed that my life had no purpose and that I had nothing to live for. Fortunately, I decided against suicide because the thought of hurting my grandparents was just too much. After all, they never gave up when they were trying to get custody of me. How could I allow all their hard work to go to waste just because of how I was feeling? To me, that would've made me selfish and a coward. Although I made up my mind that I would never commit suicide, I still wanted to die. I didn't love myself. In fact, I hated myself, and therefore I saw no reason to live.

Why live? Why live when my own mother doesn't love me, my own father is barely in my life, and nobody really cares about me? I think all this stemmed from the fact that I didn't love myself. When I began to embark on the journey to self-love, my whole outlook on life changed. No longer did

I think that I needed to be loved and accepted by everybody to have a reason to live. I realized that I don't need anything or anybody else, for that matter, to have a reason to live. See, when you start to love yourself, you learn that YOU are your own reason to live. When you come to this realization, you "move" differently — which is exactly what I did. At that point you know you are living for yourself, and no one else. When you truly love yourself, you don't do anything that you know could possibly harm you. You don't harm or mistreat yourself, and you don't allow others to mistreat you either. Genuinely loving yourself is such an amazing and beautiful thing!

I've been practicing self-love lately and I can honestly say it feels good. It feels much better than toxic relationships, depression, or suicidal thoughts. I'm literally falling in love with myself and I'm enjoying every bit of it. I'll never allow anything or anyone to take my happiness again because I love myself too much for that. I am my own reason to live, and I absolutely love it! Now don't get me wrong, there are still days when I get all in my feelings and I question my worth. However, I remind myself that I am Mya Joyce and she is smart, beautiful, and just simply amazing and nothing less. Just like loving someone else requires effort, loving yourself does too. You just have to make sure you're willing to put in that effort.

I've always been the black sheep of my family and I've come to grips with that. My family is different, to say the least. We rarely come together and when we do, I feel weird — like an outlier. Whenever family comes over, I usually stay in my room until it's time to eat. I prefer it this way because I don't like phoniness. My family has done some pretty grimy stuff to each other over the years and nobody has ever apologized. They just simply move on, act fake, and secretly hate each other.

My family isn't supportive of each other either. I can name some distant relatives who are very nice and supportive, but as for my immediate family, this is not true at all. Yes, they tend to fake like they all care and love each other so much, but I don't think that's true. They don't *really* love each other unless their definition of love is different from mine. Personally, I don't think people who love each other hate on each other or talk about each other behind each other's back. For example, my family is full of the type of people who love to see you doing good as long as you're not doing better than them. Me, on the other hand, I want everybody to win. I love seeing other people succeed because I believe we can all shine together.

If another family member is successful, they say things like "she (or he) thinks she's better than everybody else." Some of my family members have said that I think I'm better than other people, and I really don't think that way at all. I legit love everybody and I want to see everybody be great. I know writing about my family is going to ruffle some feathers, but who cares? I'm sure I'm not the only one with a dysfunctional family, and I want people who do have families like mine to know that it's not their fault and there are others in the world who can relate.

Another reason I consider myself the black sheep is because of the way my family treats me. They treat me as if I am weird, which I probably am, but it's not my fault. Maybe they're jealous because I'm going further than they ever thought I would. Who would've ever thought that the little girl whose mother was a drug addict would grow up to be one of the smartest people in our family? They probably thought that I'd never amount to anything because of who my parents are. They thought that I'd be struggling in school so when I started excelling academically, they were caught off guard.

It's kind of funny now that I think about it: the girl that everyone counted out is an *author* — ain't that something?

I know a few of my family members will be quite "salty" about this (please excuse my slang), but you have to remember that I'm still a sixteen-year-old girl, LOL). I know a few feathers will be ruffled, but I think we all need a good feather ruffling every once in a while. This was in no way meant to bash my family, because they are amazing people who've accomplished amazing things. I just think that maybe they don't realize what they're doing or maybe they just don't care, but either way I decided to speak on it because whether they like it or not, it's a part of my story. I know a lot of people don't come from perfect families, so if you come from a dysfunctional upbringing you're not alone. If you do come from a good family, don't take it for granted. Love them and appreciate them because not everybody is blessed with what you have. I would have loved to have a supportive family circle, but the lack of support has pushed me to become better — just not in the conventional way.

When I was really depressed and down in my spirits, my future was literally the only thing that kept me going. Although I was afraid of turning out like my mother, I thought that *maybe* I could be different. Teen pregnancy and drug addiction aren't hereditary, so I figured there was a chance that my life could take a different turn. I realize that my circumstances make it harder for me to succeed, which is why I always try to make sure my grades are on point. I know that the only way I can break the cycle of poverty is if I go to college and get a degree. High school diplomas aren't really cutting it anymore, so I always knew that I have to go to college.

My grades being high is the only possible way I'll be able to afford college. It's no secret that my grandparents don't have a lot of money, therefore scholarships, grants, and financial aid are my only choices. I want to avoid student loans, if possible, and for that reason I know my grades have to be up to par. At first, I had no clue what I wanted to do beyond college. This was simply because I'd never even thought I could pursue higher education until I got to high school and started believing that it was a real possibility.

Halfway through my freshman year of high school, I decided that I want to be an attorney. I still don't know what kind, but I want to major in psychology or philosophy for my undergraduate degree. I haven't yet decided on my college choices yet, but I know for sure that I'm getting out of Georgia. I want to live out of state because I desperately need a change of scenery! I want to meet new people and explore other places. Don't get me wrong, I love the South and the people down here are really nice, but I want to experience something different when I graduate.

Ideally, I want to go to college in the Northeast. I think it will be fun to finally see what life is like in the North, since my grandparents lived in that region for a long time before coming back to Georgia. As a future lawyer, I could help families who have to go through long, complicated custody battles like my grandparents. It is my desire to help people who don't have any help at all. At this moment, I think I want to be a general practice attorney because they do everything. I'm sure that will change later on, but that's what I want to do right now.

I want to major in psychology because I think the mind is a wonderful thing and I'd love to just study it. I want to study how the mind works and why it works that way. I also think philosophy would be interesting as well, but then I also sometimes think about majoring in business. One day, I want to have my own business and I know I really want to do a lot, but now I believe that I can accomplish all of my goals. After writing this book, I feel like anything is possible!

One day I even want to have a clothing boutique or something along those lines. In addition to becoming an attorney, an author, and an entrepreneur, I'd like to have my own non-profit organization. I think one day when I'm well-established in my career, then maybe I'll come back to Macon to establish a non-profit organization. I rarely see anyone in the community doing events for teen girls, so I think that's what I'd like to do with my organization in the future. I basically want to do what I'm now wishing somebody else would do in Macon, Georgia. There's almost always a party to go to in Macon, but you hardly ever hear about a girl's empowerment event or just something to uplift girls and women in the community.

Chapter 20

Finally, Free ... Almost

While I was writing this book, my mother moved out of our house. I'm honestly happy about it because maybe not seeing her everyday will help me feel better about the situation. I think we will all benefit from her moving on because she's gaining a sense of independence and we're gaining peace of mind. There were times when she caused a lot of problems in the house, and my grandparents are getting old. Therefore, I don't need them stressed out because of her. I just hope that she doesn't go crazy with this little bit of independence.

Her friends, the ones that she continually chose over us, aren't good friends at all. Instead of telling her to stay sober and become a better person, they're the ones that take her to get high and drunk. Those are the people she chooses to be around, and she doesn't even realize that they're no good for her. They use her for her money, and when she's out of money they are nowhere to be found. However, as soon as she gets her check, they magically reappear. This makes me really angry!

Although my mother moved out, she calls my grandmother every day, which I don't understand because when she was living here, she told everybody that my grandmother treated her horribly. You would've thought my grandma was evil, the way she talked about her! For that reason, I don't understand why my mother calls her every day, because she always said my grandma was such a mean, evil person. Maybe it's me, but I'd never call anybody who treated me so badly. That is another thing that makes me angry, because she was excited to move out and she was literally bragging to her friends about how she doesn't have to deal with us anymore and that she's finally free.

If my mother is so happy to finally be free from us, then she should just leave! I mean, don't call, text, or reach out to us. She was "so happy to leave," but she'll probably be back next week needing somewhere to stay because she used all her money on drugs and alcohol. She really is a mess. She even bragged about how she was happy she wouldn't have to be around us anymore because *we* got on her nerves. Girl, what? How? How did *I* get on *her* nerves? She always taunted me and put me down. Her attitude about the entire ordeal really baffled me!

My grandparents used to literally have to force her to take her medicine every night because she wasn't even responsible enough to do it. Not to mention all the stress she put us through. My grandparents literally had to crush her medicine up and put it in her food for her to take it because they couldn't trust her to take it on her own. My mother was diagnosed with schizophrenia about five years ago, which is why she is on medication. In fact, remember all those examples I gave of her acting crazy and disrespectful towards my grandparents? Almost all of those incidents were a result of her not taking her medicine. The other incidents with my mother were just because she was high or drunk.

Now don't get me wrong, I understand that she has a mental illness and that she won't fully function like a normal person, but what I won't do is blame everything on the schizophrenia because some stuff is just my mother being who she is. She enjoys getting under my skin and it makes me mad. It's like having another child in the house at times and it's stressful! I honestly don't see how my grandparents dealt with it for as long as they have, but I suppose you can put up with a lot when you really love your child.

I'm glad she moved out because now we can all get some peace. The only thing that I'm worried about is her coming back eventually. This time I need her to stay gone for good. I'm tired of the negative energy coming in and out of my life. My mother hasn't put forth any effort to change, so her moving out is a good thing. I'm sure she'll still find some way to terrorize me, but it'll be easier for me to ignore her and her antics because I no longer have to see her every day. I must say that I'm not forgiving her and giving her a clean slate just because she's moved out. Tuh! I'm still salty; I don't care. She could move to Mars and I still wouldn't forget what she's done!

I do think I'll finally be able to clear my head and really think everything over though. Maybe I will forgive her, but not because she's moved out. My forgiving her will probably come about because I don't want the toxicity that existed in her for all these years to continue to live in me, if that makes sense. The toxic person no longer lives with me, but the toxic things she left still do. One day, I want to be completely free — once and for all.

In Closing...

Being an author was something I used to dream of and now it's no longer a dream, but a reality. There were several reasons why I wanted to write this book. First and foremost, I wanted to help myself heal. While writing this book, I went through a lot of turmoil, but I truly began the healing process. Before I even started writing, I said that I wanted to be in a better place when I published this book, and to be honest, I'm not there yet. I am in a better place mentally, but not where I thought I would be. I don't know why, but I honestly thought I would have forgiven my mother by now. I thought that all of my anger would've been gone, but that's not the case.

I am handling everything better though, and I am closer to forgiving her. The things she does doesn't bother me as much anymore. I think I've finally come to terms with the fact that she may never change, and me being angry is only stressing me out instead of changing the situation for the better. While I haven't quite reached the place where I want to be just yet, I am patient with the process. Personally, I felt pressured to heal overnight sometimes, and that simply didn't happen. This book is a reminder that healing takes time. There were many nights when I cried myself to sleep because I wanted to end it all, but I didn't. I couldn't.

There were even a few panic attacks, but through it all I've become a better person. In spite of how bad I felt at times, I allowed myself to feel emotions and I faced my traumatic experiences head-on. I definitely feel much better now that I've written this book, so I've accomplished my first goal.

We often read about traumatic experiences from adults who have already overcome them, but we seldomly hear about it from children or teenagers who are still dealing with it and who haven't quite overcome their traumatic experiences yet. This is another reason why I decided to write this book. While going through my experiences, I would have liked to read a book where someone was not only talking about their past traumas, but also how they are in the *process* of overcoming them. I'm sure other people would like to read a book like that too, because there are countless individuals out there that are still working to overcome their own trauma.

I wanted this book to be written as if I was having a normal conversation with each of my readers. I wanted it to inspire and give hope, because I know how it feels to be at your lowest. I wanted to connect with each one of my readers, and I hope I did just that. I feel like I did. I wanted to tell my story and offer some advice that I would've wanted somebody to give to me.

One of the things I think about often is the kids who, like myself, have been or are currently in child protective services. If any of you are reading this, it was my goal to help you all realize that it does get better. I know what it feels like, and it's an experience that you wouldn't understand unless you've been there — it's quite traumatic. None of what happened to you is your fault. You are amazing, and you'll be stronger because of what you've been through! You're stronger than some adults. I know a few, but remember you are important, and you can be anything you want to be. I mean, look at me. I'm a published author, and if I can do it, you can too.

Another thing I wanted to accomplish with this book is to be a voice for teenagers. As I said in the opening chapter, our feelings are often ignored, and I want that to stop. The way we feel matters. Our feelings ARE valid. I hope from this point forward, every adult who reads my book will take teenagers more seriously. This book wasn't meant to bash adults either, because there are some pretty awesome adults in this world, and I'm blessed to have had as many in my life as I have. I am literally surrounded by great people; however, this world is still full of some not-so-great individuals. When we start harboring negative emotions in our teens, we often carry these emotions well into adulthood. This book is my way of saying "not so!" I refuse to be silenced, and I don't care who feels like my voice doesn't matter, because it does matter. Not only does my voice matter, but all the voices of other teenagers who are trying to heal from past experiences matter as well.

Lastly, I wanted to show that anything is possible. Where I come from, I don't know any young authors. Honestly, authors in general are very rare around Macon, Georgia. I want this to become normal. I want more people from my hometown to write books. I was honestly afraid to write this book because I'd never seen anybody *like me* do something *like this* before. At first, I didn't even think that I would be taken seriously. To anyone that has been held back by the fear of being the first, don't let anyone else stop you from going after your dreams. You can always be the first to do something, and others will be inspired by your accomplishments.

I may still have a lot of growing to do and a lot to learn in life, but I wrote an entire book, and for that I'm proud of myself. I don't know what else God has in store for me, but I am so ready to find out!

Thank you for reading and taking my journey with me!

Made in the USA
Columbia, SC
11 March 2019